Theo & Co.
TAKE 2

Theo & Co.

TAKE 2

THE SEARCH FOR THE PERFECT PIZZA CONTINUES

Theo Kalogeracos

with photography by Craig Kinder

UWAP
UWA PUBLISHING

To Polly, keep on cooking

Theo, Perth 2013

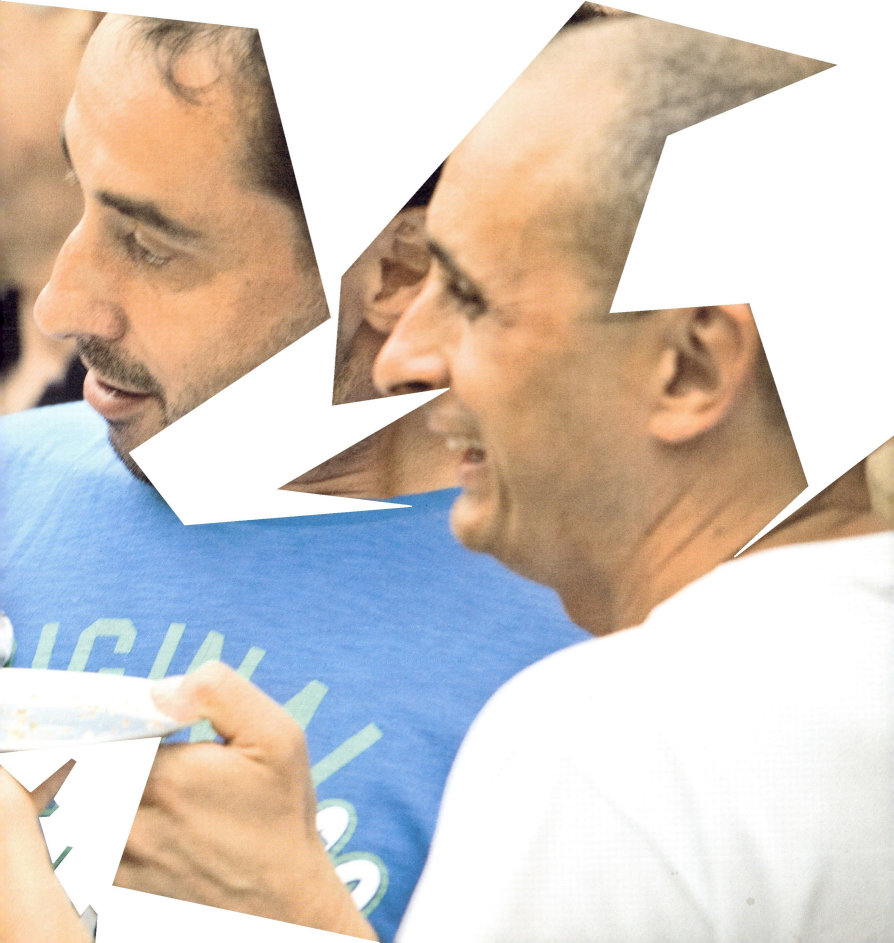

1 PIZZA PERFECTION

CLASSIC ITALIAN PIZZA	1
PIZZA-MAKING MASTER-CLASS	23
YOUR VERY OWN PIZZA OVEN	37

2 ROAD TRIP

LAS VEGAS	49
NEW YORK	63
SAN FRANCISCO	77
LOS ANGELES	85
CHICAGO	103

3 HOME SWEET HOME

BREAKFAST	111
STARTERS	119
CARNIVORE	125
SEAFOOD	151
VEGETARIAN	163
DESSERT	177

Till next time …	193
Index	194

1 PIZZA PERFECTION

This book continues the search for the perfect pizza. From Salsomaggiore to Las Vegas, New York to Los Angeles, San Francisco to Chicago, and back to Perth. I am lucky enough to have found a career that allows me this continual road trip around the globe working and eating, and it is through these experiences that I have learnt how to be a better cook and a better pizza maker. I hope to be able to tell you some of my stories, and share some new experiences and some old ways of making pizza – different styles from state to state, country to country: you can't go forward without knowing what's behind you, but with that knowledge and new experiences you truly should have the tools to create your own pizza experience, to make it your own style.

CLASSIC ITALIAN PIZZA
SALSOMAGGIORE WORLD PIZZA CHAMPIONSHIP

I could bang on about all the different style pizzas you will find throughout Italy – some made by a professional pizzaolo or by Nonna in the backyard of some village and you know what? They would all be great.

The pizza styles in Italy change from region to region and from city to city. The classic comment I hear is that all pizza should be cooked in a wood-fired oven and it should be thin like paper, that's real Italian pizza, that's what they say. But as you will see, the Italians do a pizza style called Teglia which is a pan pizza and a deep-dish pan at that! God forbid – a pizza cooked in a deep-dish pan in Italy! But it is, and you know what? It tastes great, it's a great pizza style, it's different, the toppings and flavour are also different, and you'll find this pizza style is very popular in Rome.

But, instead of giving you a history lesson or explaining all the ins and outs of pizza throughout Italy, I'm going to tell you about the most important pizza event in all of Italy.

In a small town about a three-hour drive from Milan lies Salsamaggiore, in the Parma region. This little town is surrounded by the best Parma ham and Parmesan cheese, you'll find anywhere in the world… while you are there you have got to try Parmesan butter… but that's another story.

In Salsomaggiore they hold two BIG events every year: one is the finals and the crowning of Miss Italy and the other is the World Pizza Championship. Both are held in the same stadium, this competition is taken so seriously that you would think it is life and death and you know what? For some of them it is: this one event can change a pizzeria from an average business to an overnight sensation.

You would never guess who gives the trophy to the best pizzaolo of the year. Yep, Miss Italy. Imagine that when she wins the title of Miss Italy and she is looking over her itinerary to see what she has to do over the year: fashion parade in Milan, travel to New York to meet The Donald, and yep there it is, give trophy to a pizza maker. Look at it this way, if you start working in a pizzeria and you get good at what you do, you've got a chance of getting a kiss from Miss Italy… not many people can say that.

The four categories at the Italian world pizza championship cover most styles of pizza that you will find throughout Italy, from the traditional Napoletana right up to the contemporary gluten-free pizza. Only in Italy can there be world championships dedicated to one food and fought over by 400 competitors over four days, like it is the final of the football world cup and Italy are playing. But that is how much passion they have towards making pizza.

The competition has four styles of pizza – Classica, Teglia, Senza Glutine and Napoletana STG – each with its own specific rules:

CLASSICA

This is a 13 inch round pizza. You can use whichever oven you like that they have in the competition area from wood-fired to brick, to deck, to conveyer.

The toppings on the pizza are standard Italian ingredients such as mozzarella, prosciutto, capsicum, tomatoes, bocconcini, mushroom, Pecorino, Parmesan, rocket etc.

TEGLIA

Pizza Teglia in Italy means pan pizza, and in the competition they don't care if it's square, round or rectangular, just as long as the pizza is baked in a tin, which is about 1 inch deep. It can be baked in which ever oven you like and with what ever toppings you like.

SENZA GLUTINE (GLUTEN-FREE)

It just goes to show that even though the Italians are steeped in traditions when it comes to pizza, even they acknowledge that times and diets are changing. Instead of ignoring it, they create a category in the pizza competition that, like everything else they do, is extreme. That's gutsy.

All the gluten-free dough is made in a separate room from the rest of the competition so there is no cross contamination. There is one oven dedicated to gluten-free pizzas, and no other pizza can go in this oven. All ingredients on the pizza must be gluten-free, and all utensils, cutting boards, trays, etc., are only to be used for gluten-free cooking.

The entire judging panel is actually allergic to gluten so if you stuff up guess what? You're going to make the judges sick.

NAPOLETANA STG (SPECIALITÀ TRADIZIONALE GARANTITA)

This is the hardest category in the competition, because it is so restrictive. There are only three types of pizza that can be made in this category:

1. margherita – made with tomato, fresh mozzarella, basil, extra virgin olive oil
2. margherita extra – made with tomato, fresh mozzarella from the Campania region, basil, extra virgin olive oil
3. marinara – made with tomato, garlic, oregano, extra virgin olive oil

And these three types of can only be made with 100% Napoletane ingredients and in a very specific way:

- The dough has to be made by hand
- You have to use Napoletane flour (Caputo or San Felice)
- No sugar or oil in dough
- Dough has to weigh between 250 g and 280 g, and must be stretched no smaller than 11.5 inches and no bigger than 13 inches
- The pizza must be made on a marble table
- You must sauce the pizza and place ingredients on it in a spiral motion
- The sauce has to be made from San Marzano DOP (protected designation of origin) tomatoes with only salt added
- The oven has to be 450°C
- Only cook for 90 seconds

This category really shows the skill of the pizzaolo. With everybody using the same ingredients and making the same pizzas, it's an even playing field so it's up to you to show how good your skills are at making a great pizza.

Classica

CLASSICA DOUGH

500 g Italian pizza flour
20 g fresh yeast
5 g salt
5 g sugar
330 ml warm water

Makes 5 dough balls

1. Place warm water in a bowl then break up the fresh yeast and mix using a whisk or a fork until the yeast starts to dissolve. Leave to rest for 5 minutes.

2. Add flour, salt and sugar and mix for 7 minutes. When the dough is ready cut up into 5 even balls and place in zip-lock plastic bags (like the ones you put your kids' lunches in for school) and let the dough rest for 1 hour. By putting the dough in the plastic bag, the heat from the fermentation process is captured in the dough and your pizza will end up airy and bubbly like a real Italian pizza.

3. This dough should be soft so there is no need for a rolling pin, you should be able to use the palm of your hand and some extra flour to stretch the dough to the size you want. If you use a rolling pin you will get a nice even base, which is good, but it is not a classica base. Or if you want to, you can try throwing it in the air, but remember to make sure it is spinning so it gets stretched into shape. When ready you can start putting your toppings on.

CLASSICA PIZZA SAUCE

1 tablespoon extra virgin olive oil
1 fresh garlic clove, thinly sliced
440 g tin of whole peeled tomato
7 fresh basil leaves, thinly sliced (do not chop)
pinch of salt
pinch of pepper

1. In a pan on a medium heat add the oil and garlic, when it starts to sizzle add the tomatoes, basil, salt and pepper.

2. Cook for 20 minutes and break up the whole peeled tomatoes using the back of a fork or a potato masher so they release their flavour.

3. Once cooked, let the sauce cool and it is ready for use.

1 PIZZA PERFECTION *Classic Italian Pizza*

Classica with fennel sausage

This is a simple Italian-style pizza but what makes it great is having a quality sausage, good mozzarella balls, and a nice tasting sauce – all together it will give you great flavours on a great crust.

In Italy, the mozzarella is fresh and unpasturised, which makes it a soft white cheese similar to the bocconcini you get in Australia. If you use bocconcini instead you will need 4 or 5 of the small balls for one pizza.

1 classica dough ball
2 tablespoons of classica sauce
2 fresh mozzarella balls in brine
1 Italian fennel sausage

1 teaspoon fresh parsley, chopped

Pre-heat oven to 270°C

1. With your dough stretched on the peel, place the sauce on the base and spread evenly, going close to but not quite to the edge.

2. Rip the mozzarella balls by hand and place the torn cheese pieces evenly on the pizza.

3. Cut the sausage in half and take the meat out of the skin. Throw away the skin, break the sausage meat into little pieces and scatter on the pizza.

4. Slide the pizza into the oven and cook for 3 to 5 minutes. The edges should puff up straight away and give a crispy crust and chewy center.

5. When the pizza is cooked, take it out of the oven, cut it up, sprinkle with parsley and serve.

1 PIZZA PERFECTION *Classic Italian Pizza*

Teglia

This recipe will make two teglia pizzas, 30 x 20, I use a tin that is 34 x 24 cm. You should end up with 800 g of dough, giving you 400 g per pizza.

TEGLIA DOUGH

15 g fresh yeast (or 20 g biga, see p80)
240 ml luke-warm water
500 g strong bakers flour (14% protein)
10 g salt
2 tablespoons extra virgin olive oil
4 tablespoons semolina

1. Whisk yeast into water and let sit for 5 minutes.
2. Add flour, salt and oil and mix for 10 minutes.
3. Cut the dough into two even pieces, rub oil on dough to cover and let it rest for 15 minutes under a tea towel.
4. Grease your tray with oil.
5. Sprinkle 2 tablespoons of semolina on the bench then place the dough on top and spread it out using your hand or rolling pin to the size of the tin, then place flattened dough into tin. Placing the semolina on the bench first will give you a really nice crunchy base when cooked.
6. Let the dough rest in the tray for 30 minutes before adding toppings.

1 PIZZA PERFECTION *Classic Italian Pizza*

Teglia with porcini mushrooms

There is no sauce on this pizza, I don't want the tomato sauce competing with the mushrooms for taste. This pizza is all about mushrooms — from the porcini to the fresh butted mushrooms, to the truffle oil that is drizzled at the end to give the pizza a nice shine and a beautiful aroma.

If using dry mushrooms, make sure you get rid of excess water after you have soaked them.

COOKED MUSHROOMS

3 cups fresh button mushrooms, sliced
1 tablespoon butter
1 tablespoon white wine
1 clove garlic, finely chopped
pinch of salt
pinch of pepper

PIZZA

1 teglia dough ball
100 g mozzarella, grated
1 cup fresh porcini mushrooms
1 portion cooked mushrooms
1 cup fresh ricotta

2 tablespoons shaved pecorino
3 handfuls of fresh rocket dressed in balsamic vinegar and extra virgin olive oil and seasoned with a pinch of salt
Truffle-infused oil

Pre-heat oven to 220°C

1. Melt the butter in a pan and add the garlic.
2. Add mushrooms and wine, season and cook for 3 minutes.
3. Set aside until it is time to add them to your pizza.

1. When the dough has rested in the tin for 30 minutes, place the grated mozzarella evenly on the base and then top with the porcini and cooked mushrooms, discarding excess liquid.
2. Crumble ricotta over mushrooms.
3. Place in the oven and bake for 10 to 15 minutes.
4. When cooked, take the pizza out of the tray and cut into squares.
5. Once cut, place onto a serving dish as a whole rectangle pizza and shave the Pecorino all over. Top with the dressed rocket leaves and drizzle a small amount of the truffle-infused oil all over the pizza.

Sicilian swordfish teglia

1 teglia dough ball
5 tablespoons tomato pizza sauce (I use the
    STG San Marzano tomato sauce, see p19)
100 g mozzarella, grated
200 g swordfish filets, cubed
1 tablespoon pesto
1 clove garlic, finely chopped
pinch of salt
pinch of pepper
100 g Sicilian green olives, pitted
1 tablespoon salted capers
1 tablespoon dried oregano

1 preserved Sicilian lemon (if not available just
    use a regular fresh lemon, no biggy)

Pre-heat oven to 220°C

1. With your teglia dough in the tin rested and ready, start prepping ingredients. First, in a bowl, place cubed swordfish with garlic, pesto, salt and pepper and mix. Let it sit for 5 minutes to allow the fish to absorb the marinade.

2. Spread pizza sauce over base, then top with mozzarella. Place the sword fish evenly around pizza, then add olives and sprinkle salted capers and oregano over.

3. Place in the oven and cook for 10 to 15 minutes.

4. When ready, take out of the oven, cut into squares. All this pizza needs is a squeeze of lemon to give it a real bite – the combination of tomato sauce with baked swordfish is unbeatable.

1 PIZZA PERFECTION *Classic Italian Pizza*

Senza glutine

SENZA GLUTINE DOUGH (GLUTEN-FREE)

375 g gluten-free flour (plus extra for rolling out)
1 teaspoon baking powder (this can be omitted if you like. It gives a slight aeration to the dough but it is not totally necessary)
200–250 ml aqua minerale (sparkling water, this provides a bit of aeration to the dough)

To be doubly sure that the judges didn't get sick, I made my base yeast-free and gluten-free. To get a really nice brown base on your gluten-free pizza, make sure you use an oven with really good bottom heat.

This recipe makes 650 g dough – enough for three pizzas.

Pre-heat oven to 220°C

1. Place the water in a bowl then all the ingredients on top and mix together till you get a smooth dough – it should take about 5 minutes. Roll the dough straight away or it will start to crack.

2. Using gluten-free flour on a bench and a rolling pin roll out the base to fit a 13" tray.

3. Roll the flattened dough onto the rolling pin like you do with an apple pie pastry lid then drop onto the tray, and use a knife to trim the excess that is hanging off the tray. The excess dough can be mixed into the rest of the dough to make more pizza bases.

4. Once you have rolled the dough onto the tray and trimmed it, then, for the best result, wrap the base and tray in cling wrap and put it into the freezer. This will stop the base from cracking. Leave it in the freezer for a minimum of 30 minutes (you can keep it in there for 1 month, write the date with a permanent marker on the cling wrap so you know how long it has been there).

5. When you are ready to use it, simply take it out of the freezer, do not defrost, put your sauce on, add the cheese and then the toppings. Avoid processed meats as most of them contain gluten. Usually a good roasted chicken or a hung dry Italian cacciatore sausage and prawns are gluten-free, as are fresh vegetables like capsicum, tomatoes, mushroom, eggplant and zucchini, which are all great flavours for a gluten-free pizza.

6. Place in oven and cook for 7 to 10 minutes.

1 PIZZA PERFECTION *Classic Italian Pizza*

Gluten-free vegetarian

Please make sure you have no cross contamination when you make a gluten-free pizza. From a clean bench to ingredients that have no gluten, it's not hard, you just have to be careful.

I've made this a vegetarian pizza, but you can add gluten-free meats or seafood.

1 senza glutine base
60 ml (3 tablespoons) classica pizza sauce (p4)
60 g fresh button mushrooms, thinly sliced
90 g mozzarella
80 g grilled zucchini, cut into 1cm slices
50 g roasted red capsicum, sliced
4 fresh cherry tomatoes, cut in half
pinch of salt
pinch of pepper

1 teaspoon fresh parsley, chopped

Pre-heat oven to 220°C

1. Spread the sauce evenly over the pizza base leaving 1 cm around the edge. Place mushrooms and top with mozzarella. Put the zucchini slices around the pizza along with the cherry tomato halves. Top with the roasted red capsicum and sprinkle with salt and pepper.

2. Place in oven and cook for 7 to 10 minutes.

3. When ready, cut up, sprinkle with parsley and serve.

Napoletana STG

NAPOLETANA DOUGH

750 g flour (must be from the Naples region e.g. Caputo or San Felice)
$1\frac{1}{2}$ teaspoon salt
45 g fresh yeast
360 ml water at 20°C (luke-warm)

STG SAN MARZANO SAUCE

2 tins 440 g San Marzano tomatoes
1 teaspoon sea salt

Makes 5 dough balls

1. Put water into a bowl, break yeast up and whisk it into the water. Let it sit for 5 minutes until the yeast starts to bubble.
2. Add flour and salt and mix for 7 minutes, when ready divide the dough into 5 even-sized balls, roll in flour then place each dough ball into a large zip-lock plastic bag and put in the fridge for 24 hours.
3. Remove from fridge 1 hour before you want to use the dough. When ready, place some flour on the bench, place the dough on the flour and push out and stretch to the right size – no bigger than 13 inch – place some flour on a pizza peel then put the stretched out dough onto the peel. Now you are ready for the sauce and cheese.

1. Open tins and strain excess juice – you only want the tomato pieces.
2. In a bowl crush the tomatoes to a pulp using a fork or a potato masher and mix in salt. This sauce has to be used at room temperature, that way the real tomato flavour comes out – if you use this sauce straight out of the fridge the sauce will have very little flavour.

1 PIZZA PERFECTION *Classic Italian Pizza*

Napoletana STG

For a pizza that really has only sauce and cheese on it, this is a difficult pizza to make. I want you to try something. The dough recipe will give you five dough balls: I want you to bake all five pizzas, one at a time so you can see how hard it is to make the same pizza five times, exactly the same. Try it and good luck!

To cook this pizza in 90 seconds you need a really hot oven, a wood-fired oven can get up to 450°C. If your oven doesn't get that high it will take longer, but no more than 3 minutes. You are after a soft chewy base, charred underneath from the bricks or the stone base in the oven.

1 ball Napoletana dough
3 tablespoons sauce
2 balls fresh mozzarella

3 fresh basil leaves
extra virgin olive oil to drizzle

Pre-heat oven to 450°C

1. When your dough is stretched to the right size and on the peel put the sauce on the base, then in a spiral motion (going clockwise) spread the sauce evenly around the base making sure that the only bit of dough without sauce is the crust.

2. Rip up your fresh mozzarella balls and place evenly around the pizza making sure that when it melts it covers the pizza evenly – you do not want a spot on the pizza without mozzarella.

3. Slide into the extremely hot oven and set your timer at 90 seconds and go! You must pull it out before 90 seconds or you will be disqualified.

4. When the pizza is out, slide onto a plate cut into 6 pieces, rip the basil leaves and scatter around, then, moving in the same circular motion as before, drizzle the extra virgin olive oil.

PIZZA-MAKING MASTER-CLASS

Making pizza is like building a house. When you are building a house, you lay the foundations first then you build the house on top. It's the same with a pizza: if you make a bad base, your pizza will collapse and all the ingredients will slide off. Your pizza base has to be good enough that when you are eating the pizza you don't even notice it, you are enjoying the flavours of the pizza. You know, the only time you hear someone talk about the pizza base is when it's bad, when it's too soft or chewy, or floppy.

You have to respect the craft of making dough to make a great pizza. It's not like you are cooking a soup and can taste it, adding salt or pepper as you go along. You can't do that when you are making pizza dough…if the recipe asks for 20 g of yeast you put in 20 g, if you have made a soft dough because you added too much water, it is easier to throw that dough away than it is to fix it.

The best way to make sure you do not make a mistake is to weigh and measure all your ingredients into separate bowls on your kitchen bench in the order they appear in the recipe and then check them against the recipe as you add each ingredient.

DOUGH

Flour

The biggest tip for making great pizza dough is to use the right kind of flour. It has to be plain flour but it does not matter if it is '00' (which is the finest milled of Italian flour), what you are after is a high protein level in your flour.

We call the flour we use in the industry strong bakers flour, this means the protein level in the flour is consistently over 12%. If you are looking for it in your supermarket you may have trouble finding one that high, you can find the protein percentage in the nutritional section on the packet of flour. It should be over 10%, as if it's below, it's no good for great pizza dough. The supermarkets do sell some types of pizza flour – their protein level is usually 11%. The strong bakers flour I use is 14%.

Yeast and biga

Nearly all dough recipes use instant dry yeast. It's easy to use and very good. If you want to substitute fresh yeast for dry yeast you need to double the amount of fresh yeast. Use cold water with dry yeast; with fresh yeast you need to add warm water, whisk it together and let it sit for a few minutes to activate the yeast.

Biga was used back in the day when yeast was not readily available. It is a mixture of water with flour, grapes, oats – whatever they had in the pantry that would ferment when mixed together and left to sit for 24 hours. The main reason people still use biga today is to try and get an authentic flavour to their pizza.

Temperature of the ingredients

My basic pizza dough recipe uses cold water, this is one of my golden rules (unless you are making a different style dough e.g. sour dough). It will stop your dough having hot spots which are those big air bubbles that you find on pizzas that look like volcanoes.

Flour is usually kept in the cupboard so it is already quite warm and then when you mix your dough for 10 minutes that creates a lot of friction so your dough ends up even warmer which speeds up the fermentation process. To balance this you use cold water, that way the finished dough temperature is cool not hot.

Mixing and kneading

I always put water into my mixing bowl first and add the dry ingredients on top. If you put your dry ingredients in first and then add the water,

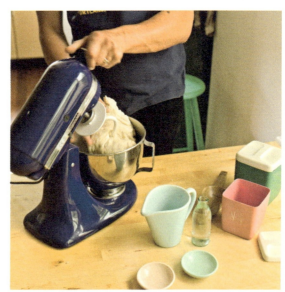

then the flour and the dry ingredients sit at the bottom of the bowl and they do not mix together properly and you always end up with excess flour in the bottom of your bowl.

When making dough in a Kitchen Aid, use a dough hook, and always mix on a low speed.

Normally when making bread dough once you have mixed the dough you cover it with a tea towel and let it double in size, but you don't do that with pizza dough. Once you have mixed it, cut it up into 200 g pieces of dough (1 kg of flour will give you eight 200 g portions) and shape them into balls and leave them to rest for just 5 minutes. This lets the dough relax so you can roll it out to the size you want. You can roll out your pizza dough to what ever size and thickness you want, but when using a rolling pin always roll from the middle of the dough and turn the dough after every roll to get a nice round pizza.

When you have rolled out the dough to the size you want, you then let it rest uncovered until it has doubled in size. By resting it at this stage you are capturing all the air from the fermentation process into the rolled out pizza dough, and by doing this you end up with a crispy airy base.

SAUCE
Some recipes in this book ask for tinned tomato cooked sauce, others ask for fresh tomato cooked sauce and still others ask for whole peeled tomato uncooked sauce, some pizzas have no sauce, and some use one of my favorites, the white sauce.

Basically what I am saying is there is no normal sauce on pizza, it all comes back to what flavour you are going for. If you want a strong tomato flavour, then use that sauce on a pizza and make the great sauce the star of the pizza.

A pizza with no sauce may seem wrong but the reason there is no sauce is so you do not draw attention away from the flavours you want your pizza to have. Sometimes tomato sauce is too strong to have on a pizza with delicate flavours; for example, if you want the flavours of oils (like in the Italian classic potato and rosemary pizza drizzled with extra virgin olive oil) or of a marinade not to be hidden under a tomato sauce, it is best to have no sauce at all.

Cream sauce always has to be put on cold, so that it slowly melts giving you a really nice creamy pizza; if you spread it on the base or use it warm it will give your pizza a soggy base.

CHEESES
Fresh mozzarella balls, grated mozzarella, blended cheese, fetta, ricotta, parmesan, goat cheese, fontina, smoked mozzarella, haloumi, soy cheese…

One cup of grated cheese (around 90 g) is the amount you should put on a 10 inch pizza. You always cheese the outer rim of your pizza first and put as little as possible in the middle; remember that the cheese on a pizza always melts from the outside into the middle.

You can use almost any cheese you like on a pizza, the one thing you have to look out for is cheese that releases to much liquid when it is cooked: all that excess water has nowhere to go except into the pizza base, which will make your pizza soggy.

Be it water or oil you don't want your pizza to go soggy. For example, fetta cheese comes in its own brine so you have to strain it to get rid of the excess water before using it. Also if you buy a soft fetta and put it on a pizza it will totally melt and you will loose the visual aspect of having fetta on a pizza. So use a firm fetta cut into nice-sized cubes, that way they will retain their shape when cooked and will look great.

Stretch curd mozzarella

I use grated stretch curd mozzarella as my base cheese on many of my pizzas. Stretch curd mozzarella sounds fancy but it just means it has gone through the process of taking a bath in hot water and as it melts mechanical arms start to stretch it. When it's finished, it's allowed to cool back into a block of cheese, and when it is hardened it is grated; that's how you get stringy mozzarella. Stretch curd mozzarella is widely available; however, if you can't find it you can use low-fat shredded mozzarella instead.

There are a few reasons why I use stretch curd mozzarella as my main cheese:

- When you eat your pizza, it has a stringy stretch that you want from pizza cheese.
- It does not have a strong flavour, which allows your ingredients to shine.
- It holds all the ingredients together on your pizza so they don't fall off as you serve it or take a bite.
- It is lower in fat than most cheeses so you don't end up with pools of extra oil sitting on your pizza, making it greasy.

Parmesan cheese

A lot of people don't like it, they say it smells like stinky socks, and they are right if you use it wrong: if you put a good 24 month aged parmesan on a pizza and cook it for 7 minutes on a high heat it will release all its oil and burn and will give off a strong smell. The best way to use parmesan is to shave some onto the pizza when it comes out of the oven – what you are after is thin shavings of parmesan hitting a hot pizza straight out of the oven, that way it will slowly start to melt and then you get a beautiful sweet parmesan cheese flavour.

Smoked mozzarella

During a competition in Las Vegas I used a smoked mozzarella that I had just discovered in Beverly Hills. It was an amazing cheese (see image to left). When I got back to Perth I realized we don't have smoked mozzarella, so I experimented and had many failures until I remembered a method the Americans call planking. On one of my trips to America I bought a very flavourful and aromomatic plank of wood that is used to smoke food. They are massive in America and everyone uses them on their BBQ or in their home oven.

What you do is you grab your plank (I used cedar) and submerge it in a sink full of tap water for 1 hour. Then you place your ball of mozzarella on it and put it in an oven that is cooling down from some other cooking. The oven needs to have cooled down to about 37°C when you use it to smoke mozzarella. Check it after 10 minutes to see that your oven is not so hot it is melting the cheese; you're not after that. What you want is for the plank to dry out and release steam, which releases the cedar taste and aroma into the mozzarella. This takes about 35 minutes and is not too difficult a process, but well worth it.

Blue cheese

It's best to crumble blue cheese over the pizza after it has been cooked. If you cook the pizza with the blue cheese on it you will lose all the great flavours and creaminess of the blue cheese; by crumbling it on the pizza after it is cooked, the cheese heats up slightly and melts just enough to release flavours and textures that are amazing.

Haloumi

This is a very under-used ingredient for pizzas. It is a Cypriot cheese that is heated up when it is made and mixed like a pizza dough is. When cool, it is cut up into small slabs that are grilled on the BBQ or in a frying pan. It doesn't melt; it grills up beautifully and has a great texture when eaten.

Soy cheese

This is a really good substitute for people allergic to dairy and you can find it in most supermarkets. It does burn when used on a pizza, so the trick is to grate your block of soy cheese and put it in the freezer. It will last for about 2 months frozen. When you need to use it on your pizza, simply put it on frozen. That way it will slowly defrost in the oven as the pizza is cooking and at the end of the cooking time the soy cheese will start to go brown but not burn.

TOPPINGS

Less is more.

That is a difficult rule to follow, but use it as your guideline. You don't need ten ingredients on a pizza to make it taste great. In fact, with that many ingredients all the flavours get lost and you don't know what you are eating. If you have three or four strong ingredients, that is what you will taste, so pick an ingredient and make it the star on your pizza.

Say it with me one more time: LESS IS MORE. The placing of toppings on a pizza is dictated by the ingredient. Sun-dried tomatoes and some cured meats should go under the cheese so they don't burn. Fresh tomatoes, capsicum and onions go on top as they need cooking, fresh herbs get put on when the pizza has come out of the oven and is cut up.

And when you think about toppings, think about flavours and textures: you want to create something that is unique, balanced, memorable. Also think about eye appeal – it is everything. We all eat with our eyes first, so if it looks good you are half way there, all you need is for it to taste good and you've got a great pizza. If you look at any great pizza from, New York to Perth, the ones that you remember and the ones that really work are the ones with great tasting ingredients. For example, the Birds of Tokyo pizza really only has one main ingredient, chicken, the chicken is marinated in teriyaki sauce then placed on top of the cheese on the pizza, sesame seeds are sprinkled on top of the chicken so when the pizza goes into the oven, the sesame seeds toast giving a

1 PIZZA PERFECTION *Pizza-making master-class*

nice nutty flavour to the pizza. When the pizza is cooked and taken out of the oven and cut, it is decorated with pickled cucumbers which are crunchy with a slight sour tang – this is a perfect balance to the strong teriyaki flavour. Then you drizzle Japanese mayonnaise onto each piece and you have your cherry on top. The mayo makes the pizza creamy so even though it is a simple pizza there is so much depth of flavour. A perfect example of each ingredient bringing another element to the pizza with each ingredient elevating the pizza from good, to great, to amazing.

Your toppings don't have to be expensive, but they do have to be bold in taste and flavour, giving the pizza a great balance, which is what makes a memorable pizza moment.

STORING

When the pizza base is ready for the toppings, you can do what I do and put them into the fridge ready for when you need them. By putting your rolled out bases into the fridge you are stopping the fermentation process. You can store them for up to six hours in the fridge, that way when it comes to baking your pizzas all you have to worry about is putting the ingredients on top and cooking your pizzas.

When having friends over for a pizza party I like to enjoy myself – sitting down, eating pizza; not rolling dough out like a mad man trying to keep up with the hungry ones. So rolling them earlier and keeping them in the fridge let's me enjoy the night as well.

You can use your pizza bases straight out of the fridge, because the heat of the oven will re-activate the yeast.

You can also freeze the topped pizzas before they are cooked. Let's say you make the dough recipe that makes eight 10-inch pizza bases and you only need one for that night. If you are going to make eight and only use one, you may as well go to the whole effort. Get or make some good pizza sauce, buy a bag of grated cheese and make eight pizzas, freeze seven and eat one. I promise you that one night, when you are in a rush for dinner and you open the freezer and catch sight of the frozen pizzas you made, it's going to put a smile on your face.

You can freeze a pizza with any kind of toppings, but I try to avoid using any watery ingredients. Most vegetables are okay but I don't like to freeze fresh tomatoes as they are full of water and when you start to cook the frozen pizza all that extra water will make the base soggy.

Freezing pizza is as easy as 1–2–3

Make up your pizza, but instead of putting it into the oven, cling wrap it and put it into the freezer. You always cling wrap the pizza and the pizza tray all together, if you put it into the freezer without the tray it will not have a flat surface to sit on and then it will freeze to what ever shape it is sitting on.

After 12 hours take the frozen pizza out of the freezer unwrap it and take the tray away, then re-wrap it with a double layer of cling wrap to prevent freezer burn.

Write the date that you put the pizza into the freezer in permanent marker and from that date you have three months to eat it.

Cooking frozen pizza

Place the frozen pizza straight into the oven, that way the excess water from freezing starts to evaporate from the heat in the oven, and the base will be crispy.

If you are using a counter-top pizza oven, place the frozen pizza into the oven with top and bottom elements both on for 10 minutes, then

1 PIZZA PERFECTION *Pizza-making master-class*

turn off the bottom element and use the top for another 5 minutes and you will have a beautiful crispy fresh pizza in 15 minutes.

If you are using a household oven, pre-heat your oven for 20 minutes at 220°C or as hot as your oven gets making sure the fan is off – you want a nice solid dry heat. If you have the fan on, it will cook your pizza too fast and it will look cooked on the bottom and top but it will be raw in the middle. It should take about 20 minutes for a frozen pizza to cook in a household oven.

At home I have one of those counter-top pizza ovens and when my son invites some friends over for a swim in the pool, I plug in the oven outside (I can't have a bunch of kids eating and making a mess in the house) and give them some pre-made frozen pizzas. That way, when they get hungry all they have to do is put a frozen pizza into the oven and it will be ready in about 10 to 15 minutes. I keep telling them that they have to wait 20 minutes before they can jump back into the pool but they don't listen, they are all too excited.

Imagine jumping around the pool, having pizza cooking in the oven, it doesn't get any better for them or for you. Just think: no mess, no fuss and happy kids.

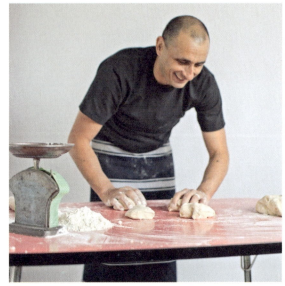

Basic pizza dough and sauce

DOUGH

1 kg strong bakers flour
20 g dry yeast
10 g salt
10 g caster sugar
660 ml cold (not chilled) water

SAUCE

7 fresh tomatoes, as red as you can get them
2 cloves fresh garlic, finely chopped
1 teaspoon salt
$\frac{1}{2}$ teaspoon pepper
1 teaspoon fresh parsley, chopped

Makes 8 dough balls

This method helps develop a 'feel' for making dough by hand, but the recipe can also be made using a mixer – just follow the instructions on p23.

1. Start by mixing all the dry ingredients together and creating a well in the centre. Carefully pour 600 ml of water into the well and gradually incorporate the water into the flour mixture. It will take three to four minutes for the dough to come together. The remaining 60 ml of water is only added if necessary, depending on the gluten content of the flour.
2. Knead the dough for about 10 minutes, but avoid watching the clock and try instead to develop a feel for what is right. A well-kneaded ball of dough should be smooth and springy, yet soft. At this stage it should be possible to stretch the dough quite thinly, so it is translucent when held up to the light.
3. Divide into eight even-sized balls and leave to rest under a tea towel for 10 to 15 minutes.
4. Roll, throw or stretch the dough with the palm of your hand to the desired size. A 200 g dough ball will make a 10 inch (25 cm) pizza. Make all the bases as quickly as you can. If you don't have enough pizza trays, you can place them on non-stick paper sprinkled with semolina – these can be stacked in threes and kept in the fridge until you are ready too cook. I do this when I make wood-fired pizzas which are cooked on the hot bricks without a tray.
5. You are now ready to start creating you own pizzas. Experiment with toppings, imagine what flavours will go well together and then try it out.

1. Using a coarse grater, grate the tomatoes into a bowl discarding the skin, add garlic, salt and pepper and mix.
2. Put the tomato sauce in a pot and simmer on medium heat for about 30 minutes – you want the sauce to reduce to half the size it was when you grated the fresh tomatoes.
3. When finished, stir in the parsley and let the sauce cool down before putting it on the pizza.

This sauce will keep for seven days in a sealed container in the fridge.

TOSSING PIZZA DOUGH

The world champion of pizza dough tossing is my friend Tony Gemignani and he has won so many awards that nobody even comes close. Over the years he has tried to teach me but I'm not that great.

Back in the day before they had machines to roll out pizza dough or even rolling pins, they used to throw the dough in the air. It was their way of making the dough get bigger in size without ripping. Because, as you throw your pizza dough up in the air, spinning it clockwise, the dough levels out and as it's spinning it stretches, and as it comes down it starts to relax. By doing this three or four times your pizza dough keeps getting bigger and bigger, plus your friends will be impressed. Your dough needs to be soft so I would suggest you use the Napoletana STG dough.

1. Place flour on the bench and put your dough ball on the flour. Sprinkle some on top then, using the palm of your hand and turning at the same time, flatten the dough as much as you can.
2. Shake off excess flour, place the flattened dough ball on the top of your hands covering your knuckles then lower your hands to about your nose level and flick the dough up with a slight twist of the wrist making the dough spin clockwise, or anticlockwise if you are a left handed.
3. Catching the dough is as important as throwing it: this is where you can tear your dough. When the dough is coming down from the throw, place your hands up in the air ready to catch the falling dough with the back of your hands, make sure your fingers are tucked under and pointing down. Do not and I mean *do not* catch it with your fingers pointing to the sky – your fingers will go straight through the dough and ruin your pizza base.
4. Once you have reached the size of pizza you want, place some semolina on your pizza peel, place the stretched dough on top, and its now ready for your ingredients.

YOUR VERY OWN PIZZA OVEN

No matter what type of oven you use, two rules apply: time cooks, temperature colors – the more toppings you have on your pizza, the longer it needs to cook, so you need a lower heat. A pizza with only a few toppings (like the Napoletana STG) can cook faster at a higher heat.

There are so many pizza ovens out there: electric, counter-top, gas, brick, conveyor, deck, wood-fired, clay. Like every chef has a favourite knife, every one has their favourite pizza oven. So you just need to find one that suits you.

Gas outdoors oven
These ovens have a maximum effective temperature of 250°C. Over the years I have used gas pizza ovens a lot. Because they are so easy to set up, I often use them in my cooking demonstrations. You just press the button to ignite, and the oven is ready for cooking about 30 minutes later, it's that simple. The other great thing about gas pizza ovens is that you have full control over the temperature and you get a consistent temperature without having to do anything.

When you want to cook your pizza, put it on the middle shelf of the oven. Check it after 7 minutes to see if you need to move it. If your base needs more browning, it needs bottom heat, so put it on a lower shelf. If the toppings need more cooking place it on the top shelf.

Domestic oven (electric or gas)
These ovens have an effective temperature of 220°C, which is good enough to cook most pizzas in this book. Cook your pizza with the fan off, this creates a solid heat and should cook your pizza in 10 to 12 minutes. Cook your pizza on the middle shelf of the oven and check it after 7 minutes to see if you need to move it. If your base needs more browning, it needs more bottom heat, so put it on the lower shelf. If the ingredients and the cheese need more cooking place it on the top shelf. (If you are using a tile or stone in your oven, pre-heat it in the oven for 30 minutes before sliding your pizza onto it).

Counter-top pizza oven
These have a pre-set temperature and are really easy to use, as there is no pre-heating. An average pizza should cook in 10 minutes and a frozen pizza in 15 minutes.

Wood-fired oven, brick oven, Mexican volcanic clay oven
All these ovens can reach temperatures of up to 250°C–300°C. The two rules that apply to all ovens, apply especially to wood-burning ones: time cooks, temperature colours. So the more ingredients you use, the longer the cooking time and the lower the heat. An outdoor pizza oven is no longer just an oven, it is a magnet. Start your outdoor oven, tell people you are having an outdoor pizza party and you watch, everybody comes. That is the beginning of a great day: friends, family, food, good times.

Everything I know about wood-fired ovens I have learnt from my uncle Caesar in his Balcatta backyard. He may be in his eighties and a pain in the arse sometimes, but what he knows about wood-fired ovens is worth learning.

I've been delaying getting a wood-fired oven built in my backyard forever. I have always felt that if I got one, I wanted to be able to use it properly, and to do that I needed to know more about the craft of using an outdoor wood-fired oven.

Caesar had one built in his backyard in the '80s – it's the wrong shape, has cracks all over it and no thermometer, but the way he uses it is amazing.

Over the years of family meals, I've been able to stand next to him and learn. He let me burn my hands then and now he watches me while he sits there complaining about Berlusconi.

Together we have roasted meats, made breads and pizzas. All I know about wood-fired ovens he has passed on to me and I'm going to pass his tips on to you, along with some of my own.

CHOOSING YOUR OVEN

What size oven suits you? When shopping around for your oven, take your biggest baking tray with you, and use that as your measurement guide. Take into consideration room for the fire and also room to bake other foods at the same time, you don't want to put a roast in the oven for two hours and not be able to use the oven because there is no oven floor space left.

Use my pizza guide as to what size oven you should buy or build. I have taken into consideration space for the fire and a small baking tray being used at the same time as the pizzas, the size of the pizzas are 12 inches (30 cm):

- 2 pizzas in the oven at the same time, you will need a small oven
- 3 pizzas in the oven at the same time, you will need a medium oven
- 4 pizzas in the oven at the same time, you will need a big oven

Are you going to use the oven every day, replacing your home oven? If you are, then a smaller that heats up faster is the way to go.

If you are mainly going to use it with lots of family and friends around, then you will need a bigger oven to be able to cook for lots of people at your party.

BUILDING YOUR OVEN

There are two main building materials used in building wood-fired ovens: individual refractory bricks or a refractory dome.

Individual refractory bricks

These are trimmed and laid in a traditional dome-shaped oven; these ovens are mortared together (with a lot of skill) using a high-heat, low-expansion refractory mortar cement.

Once the floor of the oven is built, it needs to be cured (dried out) this takes about seven days. Then it is time to light the virgin fire (p41) and then your oven is ready to use.

If you are a good handyman, this could be a great DIY job for you. For the rest of us who pay a handyman to do jobs around the house, keep away!

Refractory dome

This oven has evolved with technology, and it suits today's lifestyle. These ovens are made from one piece of high-heat, cast refractory dome. This type of oven has the ability to absorb heat at a rapid rate. The pre-made refractory dome is placed on top of a reinforced slab of hebel (a high-performance aerated concrete with great thermal holding capacity), which has a layer of ceramic insulation board on top. That is topped with a 25 mm layer of refractory bricks which will be the floor of the oven. The dome is insulated with a ceramic blanket and a thin layer of high heat mortar – those extra layers over the refractory dome help the oven to trap heat, which helps the heat soak into the oven quickly.

This oven is built in about three hours and is ready for the virgin fire straight away and after going for three hours with a slow and steady fire at about 200°C it's ready to be used.

This is the modern wood-fired oven.

Remember this: if you are building or buying a wood-fired oven, the best ones are ovens that have the best insulation. It is not about how thick your refractory bricks are; it's about your oven retaining heat. A good ceramic insulation board under the floor bricks is a must, this will give you a hot oven floor which will help you get a crispy pizza crust every time.

USING YOUR OVEN

Virgin fire

The first time you start a fire in your oven make sure you heat up the oven gradually – don't fill it up with wood and start an inferno. The virgin fire releases water that is trapped in the refractory dome.

In the middle of your oven floor place seven small pieces of firewood (kindling). They should be no fatter than the thickness of your finger. Also place two pieces of good dry hard firewood, and use a few firelighters to make your fire start easily.

Let your oven heat up 50 degrees every hour over the course of a day by slowly adding more wood, that way the oven will heat up evenly helping it to dry out and prevent your oven from cracking.

When this is done, your oven is ready for everyday use.

Firing up your oven

The main rule is don't have your fire under your flue hole – if you do, all the heat will go straight up the flue and out of the oven, wasting wood and heat.

Position the fire at the back of the oven or to one side, depending on the shape of your oven; this leaves you plenty of oven floor space for your pizzas or baking trays. If you always start the fire to one side of the oven, it will crack the dome as there is too much heat too close to the roof of the oven.

When the fire is positioned correctly, the heat will go up, hit the roof of the oven and reflect back down to the oven floor, soaking the floor bricks.

The fire should take up as little room on your oven floor as possible.

A way to tell if your oven is ready, is after the fire has died down and you have glossy coals, you will see patches of clean white spots appear on the roof of your oven. The patches will slowly join up together and you will have a white roof dome: that means the heat has soaked into the core and the oven is ready to go.

Soaking the core of your oven gives you hours of cooking time without a flame, just coals. When your oven starts to cool, just add one piece of wood at a time to bring the temperature up, don't throw heaps of wood in, if you do that, you will get lots of flames which will just burn your food before it's ready.

When the bricks are soaked with heat, then you are ready, remember you are cooking with heat not fire.

Heating your oven for 3 to 4 hours will give you a hotter oven for longer.

Gas in a wood-fired oven

I know it sounds wrong, but it works, and it works really well. You can buy a gas kit that can be installed into your wood-fired oven; this gives you two types of fuel to heat up your oven. The idea is that all you do is turn on the gas, push a button and you've got a fire. Let your oven get to the right temperature, it's the same time as when the roof of your oven turns white, at this stage you can continue to use the oven only on gas without a problem. If you want some smoke in your oven

or some coals to give it some authenticity, you can place a few pieces of good dry firewood, which will light up by themselves just from the heat in the oven.

Wood/fire logs

If you are like me, buying pre-packed and pre-dried fire wood in a bag is a great way to get a variety of good dry wood for your oven. The other option that is available to you is what they call SMART FUEL, ecologs. They are made from hardwood woodchips compacted together to give you a log that can be broken into bits by hand to start the fire and then added to a fire to maintain the heat. Ecologs burn hotter than dried fire wood as their moisture content is only 10%. They are a pricier option but with today's lifestyle and our future to look out for, they make a lot of sense.

The best burning wood is called seasoned or dry wood. Green wood (freshly chopped trees) holds about 50% of its weight in water, which is why it's no good for your oven. If you add freshly chopped wood to the fire, steam comes out of the wood and does not heat up your oven. If you are cooking with unseasoned wood it will make your bread and pizzas soft due to too much steam in the oven.

Jarrah is my favourite wood to use for a fire as, when dried properly, it gives you a solid heat and it burns slowly.

Drying out wood is essential to having a clean burning oven. When you dry out wood you are reducing its water content, which will make your oven more efficient.

When drying wood, you will notice the wood split and warp, that is part of the drying process.

At home in the hills, the way we dried wood was to leave it out in the open for a year, even during winter when it was raining. Over the course of the year, honey-coloured sap will ooze out of the wood and, after the wood has been outside for a winter and summer, it can be stored in a dry shed.

When the wood has been dried out and most of the moisture and sap has gone, you will find that the wood burning in your oven does not release excess smoke.

Temperatures

Time cooks, temperature colours. Those are the rules, follow them.

For example, if you are cooking a 1 kg roast,

it should take 1 hour, so you will need a low temperature to cook your roast for 1 hour.

If you are cooking a pizza, it should cook in about 5 minutes, so you need a higher temperature than what you'd use for your roast.

A trick my uncle Caesar taught me was that when you have been cooking pizzas on one side of the oven for a while, the heat from the bricks gets absorbed by the pizza so a pizza that used to take 5 minutes to cook, now takes 10 minutes. So use a shovel to move the coals in the oven from one side to the other, then use a damp mop to clean the floor of the oven. This ensures you will not have ash all over your pizza base. The bricks that were under the coals can now be used as they are hotter and your five minute pizzas are back.

Moving the fire around is a bit of hard work but it makes great sense when you get the hang of it.

These are some guides to follow when baking in your oven:
- Bread (loaf), 220°C, 20 minutes
- Pizza, 250°C, 5 to 7 minutes
- Roast 1 kg, 170°C, 60 minutes
- Apples, 200°C, 60 minutes
- Potatoes, 200°C, 60 minutes
- Fish (whole) 1.5 kg, 180°C, 40 minutes
- Chicken (whole) 1.5 kg, 220°C, 60 minutes

Thermometer

You need one. Make sure that the thermometer you buy is for extreme heat, as your oven will get up to 600°C – not that you will be cooking at that temperature; if you do, you will be cooking charcoal.

To make your life easier it makes sense to have two thermometers.

One that is a dial with a long prong that you build into your oven; either in the wall of the oven or on the door – this will give you a permanent oven temperature reading.

The other is a self-standing thermometer that you place in the oven to check your central heat and then remove.

All ovens have hot spots and cold spots; using a thermometer takes out all the guesswork of where these spots are lurking.

Using a door to your advantage

Baking bread in a wood oven is a lot easier when you use a door on your oven. A door stops the air from coming in and changing the temperature. You will get a solid heat in your oven by shutting the door when the bread goes in, this will help the bread get a real kick in the oven and give you a crusty loaf.

Baking a leg of lamb slowly at a consistent temperature is also achievable by using your thermometer to gauge the temperature of your oven, and using the oven door to control the heat.

Adding aromatics and smoking foods in your wood-fired oven

When you are baking in your oven you can add any kind of herbs or spices to the coals to get an aromatic smell and taste into the food. It's great to use oily herbs like rosemary that release a great smell that infuses flavour into whatever you are cooking.

You can add any flavours you like that will go with what you are cooking. Some great combinations are:
- Cinnamon stick + baked custard apples
- Garlic + fish
- Orange or lemon peel + pork
- Fresh oregano + baked onions
- Bay leaves + chicken
- Rosemary + lamb

Smoking foods

At the end of the day, when you have finished baking and your oven is cooling down, it is the perfect time to use your oven to smoke foods.

There are two ways to smoke foods: hot smoke and cold smoke.

Hot smoke

The ideal temperature for hot-smoking foods is 74°C to 85°C. Hot smoking is generally indirect cooking – this means you are cooking raw food for a long period of time with a low heat still burning in the oven. Smoking food in this way means you are both cooking and infusing the food with a smokey flavour.

Some foods that are hot smoked:
- Salmon steaks (smoke for about 45 minutes)
- Pork roll (smoke for about 3 hours)
- Brisket (also called prime beef cut, smoke for about 5 hours)

Cold smoke

When your oven has cooled down to about 38°C, you can use it to cold smoke foods that have already been cooked. Cold smoke does not cook your food, it will only infuse it with the smokey flavour. The time it takes to cold smoke foods depends on the thickness of the food. Some cooked foods that you can cold smoke are:
- Chicken pieces (smoke for 30–40 minutes)
- Mozzarella, whole ball (smoke for about half an hour) (p27)
- Cacciatore (Italian dried sausage, smoke for up to 1 hour)
- Cheddar cheese (smoke for 30–40 minutes)

Cooling your oven down and cleaning it

Do not just finish cooking and walk away from your oven.

When you have finished cooking, spread the remaining coals evenly around the oven floor, this will help the oven cool down evenly, and it will cook off any food that's dropped onto the oven floor.

The next day when your oven is cold, shovel all of the ash out of the oven, then, using a mop that only gets used in your oven (do not use any detergent), wash the floor of the oven three times changing the water each time.

Now your oven is ready for next time.

Tools of the trade
- Scraper
- Peel
- Brush
- Poker/puller
- Oven gloves
- Mop

2 ROAD TRIP

The first time I went to America was for a pizza competition held in New York in 2004. I'd never thought of going to America – Europe and Asia always interested me more, and that's where I liked going. My first trip to the States was a real love–hate relationship. It was only after coming home and missing what I had seen that I said to myself, I have to go back more often. There was so much to take in all at once, from seeing the Hollywood sign when landing in LA, to standing in Times Square at 3 am because I couldn't sleep. It was surreal.

On that first trip I had eaten some good food but mostly bad, had drunk all bad coffee – it was a short trip, successful, but a blur. Since then I've been back over a dozen times, mostly competing in Las Vegas. Sometimes to teach pizza cooking classes, other times to do TV appearances or to judge pizza competitions. From New York, Brooklyn, New Jersey to LA, San Francisco, Sacramento, down south to Houston and Austin, Texas (which rocks) and finally Cleveland, Ohio and Louisville Kentucky – nice place and great friends there.

Over time I've found the good food and the great coffee shops, I even know which record stores sell rare vinyl. In LA with a GPS I almost feel like a local! I go to the States three or four times a year. My feelings towards America have changed and the reason for that is the people. I've been invited to their houses where I now feel like part of the family and made life-long friends. Sometimes I meet people for the first time and three hours later they are taking me to a restaurant. I even think I could live there if I found a place that has the same weather as Perth and I could move my whole family over.

LAS VEGAS
DO WHAT YOU LOVE AND GIVE IT YOUR ALL

Viva Las Vegas baby, there's no other place like it.

After years of entering pizza competitions in Australia and winning a few, I became a judge in Australia. Then I got the chance to be the first Australian to be invited to the Pizza Today Expo in Vegas where they hold the world's best pizza maker competition. You can't just rock up and say I make great pizza; you have to be a winner in your own country to compete. When you are in this kind of competition you cannot help but learn and get better at what you do. You are surrounded by the world's best, and I have always loved competing for that very reason.

Now I'm a judge in Vegas, so every year I get to sit down and eat some great pizzas, but as good as that is, I would rather have a dirty apron on and be on the other side of the bench competing.

LAS VEGAS PIZZA TODAY EXPO

I was so excited to head to the Pizza Today Expo as it was the first time that my wife, Liz, was coming to America with me. It was a great chance for me to show her great new places and drive her around (and drive her crazy). She had always wanted to come, but with work, our son Chaz and life, she was always too busy to get away, but this time it was different we had booked the tickets and she was coming.

We were packing our bags, which means Liz was packing and I was watching. She always packs my bags – that way I don't forget anything. If I pack by myself, I just make sure I've got my iPod, headphones, ticket – and then I'm ready to go.

There was work to be done as well on this trip. I had arranged to go to some of my favourite pizzerias and some new ones in LA, then drive on to Vegas to eat more pizza, drive down to San Fran to eat more pizza, and then drive back to LA to come home about 5 kg heavier. I was doing research by eating pizza, talking to chefs, looking into new pizza kitchens and drinking some wine (it's a hard life, I know, but some poor guy has to do it).

We were also going to Vegas for the Pizza Today Expo where I would be competing in a pizza competition, so I would need certain clothing and equipment. It is no big deal to Liz when I compete (you have to remember I've been entering competitions for more than ten years, so for her it was just another one). This is how our conversation went when Liz was packing:

T: I need my Doc Martens.
L: They're not coming – too heavy and bulky.
T: What am I going to wear?
L: Just wear your everyday black sneakers.
T: What about my chef jacket and chef pants?
L: No, takes up too much room.
T: What am I going to wear when I compete?
L: What? Am I your mother?
L: …a black T-shirt
L: …and black jeans
T: But it runs over three days, you have only packed two T-shirts.
L: That's all you need
L: Aprons, two, OK?
T: OK.

So we get to Vegas and I'm in the first round making the Strawberry Fields pizza wearing my black jeans, black T-shirt and a nice clean mini apron (not a proper apron, but one that will take up the smallest amount of room in the suitcase).

Liz came to the expo that day for about an hour.

The next day I'm in Round 2 and I'm wearing the same black jeans and shoes with a new black t-shirt that says ZOO York and a new mini apron. I look like an idiot. Liz doesn't even show up that day – too busy shopping. Lucky for me that she is though.

I ring her late in the afternoon with good

news: I'm into the final but I need her to get me a new black t-shirt and apron.

Third day is the finals. I'm wearing a brand-new-out-of-the-pack-with-the-fold-lines-still-there $30 black American apparel T-shirt, same black jeans, same black sneakers and a dirty apron turned around so it looks clean.

You gotta love the girl! Now we laugh about it, she says what was the big deal with what you wore? You won. She's right (she usually is).

Wednesday 3 March 2010,
Las Vegas Pizza Today Expo
Today is the day of the non-traditional competition – that means anything goes. There are at least seven groups in this competition, and I'm in the open category, which is pizza champions from around the world, and we all have one chance to impress the judges. Basically you make your pizza, give it to the officials who then take it to the judges who are in a separated room so they cannot see who made the pizza. Only the winner from each category goes through to the next round along with two wild cards. I'm making a dessert pizza. I've been making dessert pizzas for fifteen years (it's my pastry chef background, I can't help it) and the one I'm making is called Strawberry Fields. It's a new one, not even on the menu back home at the pizzeria (yet).

At the end of a long day they call out the winners of each of the categories and the two wildcards. I won in my group, but the score of the Strawberry Fields pizza is fourth overall. At least I'm into the next round. I didn't know if the judges were going to throw the pizza back at me or if they would like it, so I'm happy to progress to the next round. The score was good but not great, so I have to improve it if I want to stand a chance.

Thursday 4 March 2010,
Las Vegas Pizza Today Expo
I'm the first competitor in the kitchen – not even the security guards are there to check my badge. I start making my dough, then I start to think about how to improve the pizza: the almond cake mix part of the pizza is good, nothing to change there. The strawberry jam I made yesterday was slightly runny, so this time I should take more care and make it thicker. The extra liquid yesterday made the pizza slightly soggy.

In the end, there were two moments that made this pizza great. As I was toasting the almond flakes I added sugar and butter to caramelise them and then Phillip (you're the man) told me how he whisks up an egg white, puts his pecans in it, puts them on baking paper and bakes them in the oven till they're nice and light brown. When they cool down you crumble them up for a real crunchy nut. It's a risk trying something you haven't done before in the finals of a competition – but no guts, no glory. Phillip was spot on, they tasted fantastic.

The other thing the pizza needed was another colour. It looked great with the almond mix, icing sugar, strawberry sauce, caramelised almonds and vanilla ice cream, but it needed something else: mint (thanks Dominick). Mint and strawberries go so well together but I couldn't find any at the expo kitchen. As I was about to get in my car and head to the supermarket, which would have cost me half an hour of driving around instead of concentrating on cooking, I had one of those moments that makes all us pizza makers around the world one big family. Ade from New York, who I only met two days ago, comes up to me and says, 'I hear you are looking for mint' and he hands me his container of fresh mint. I'm blown away and I kiss and hug him, I was that excited and you know what? Without the mint, I don't think my Strawberry Fields dessert pizza would have won in the second round.

2 ROAD TRIP *Las Vegas*

Strawberry fields

STRAWBERRY JAM

100 g caster sugar
200 ml water
1 teaspoon vanilla paste
300 g fresh strawberries – washed, top cut off and diced into small pieces

DESSERT PIZZA

1 basic pizza dough ball – rolled, rested & ready
1 cup almond meal
½ cup caster sugar
1 large egg
1 tablespoon melted butter
3 fresh strawberries – cut into quarters

icing sugar
2 scoops vanilla bean ice-cream
2 tablespoons strawberry jam
1 tablespoon toasted or caramelised almonds
fresh mint

Pre-heat oven to 220°C

1 Place the water in a non-stick pot and bring to boil, then lower to a simmer and add the caster sugar. Whisk till all the sugar is dissolved, then add strawberry pieces. Stir and scoop up some of the sugar syrup and pour it back into pot, it will be runny; when you can do that and it drizzles off the spoon into the pot like thick then your jam is ready.

2 It usually takes about 30 minutes to cook on a low heat.

3 I usually put the jam in a bowl and when it's cool, I cover it with cling wrap and put it in the fridge. It will last about two weeks, but you will use it before then on ice-cream, toast, and the Strawberry Fields pizza, of course.

1 To make the frangipanie mix, place almond meal and caster sugar in a bowl. Mix and set aside.

2 In another bowl whisk up egg, add frangipanie mix and pour melted butter on top (so the hot butter doesn't cook the egg). Mix and spread onto pizza base. Place eight strawberry pieces on the outside circle and four in the middle and bake for 7 minutes.

3 To serve, cut into eight pieces, dust with icing sugar, and place some ice-cream, almonds and strawberry jam plus mint on each piece.

Friday 5 March, Black Box

There are just four finalists left: two competitors from the traditional pizza-making category and two from the non-traditional pizza-making category. Not only did we have to win our division, we also had to win our categories to end up in the top four, and now we have the Black Box.

The Black Box part of the competition lets you have 40 ingredients and 90 minutes to present a pizza to the judges. If you drop the pizza or stuff it up in any way, too bad, game over. If you win, you are crowned the Pizza Maker of the Year.

As I was standing at my prep bench starting to get my pizza ready, Jeremy White, the Chief Editor from *Pizza Today Magazine*, comes up and, with a camera man in my face and a microphone, he says: 'Chef Theo you are the only contestant out of the four without an assistant'. That's when I looked up to see what was going on around me. I was so in the moment of making pizza that I could have been back in Perth making a pizza for a customer. I didn't need help, I was doing what I've been doing for fifteen years: trying to make the best pizza I can make.

We have one hour to go.

I don't like many of the ingredients that are in the Black Box. I am looking for something creative and different, but there are no inspiring ingredients, just the run-of-the-mill onions, tomatoes, capsicum, etc. The only rule is that we all have to use chicken on the pizza, apart from that, we can use anything in the box. As I look at the ingredients, I notice some freshly made pesto…chicken and pesto together: you can't go wrong. The chicken looks dry as it has been sitting for a while, so I need to add something to give it some moisture, then I see some fresh cream, perfect! I dice the chicken and mix it with the cream and pesto in a bowl – so the chicken will soak up the cream and make it moist and the pesto will coat it, creating some great flavours. Leaving the chicken in the bowl to marinate, I get cracking on getting the other ingredients ready for the pizza.

One chopped red onion into a pan with a little olive oil, salt and pepper…cook it down to a nice light-brown colour over a low heat…add a teaspoon of brown sugar and with a slight toss to mix, the onion is beginning to caramelise and will be fully caramelised once it has been cooked on the pizza.

Next, a pan on the heat with a knob of butter, chopped mushrooms, salt and pepper. After a few minutes the mushrooms are cooked, and I toss through a handful of freshly chopped parsley.

At this stage I stop and look at what I have in front of me, while I arrange the pizza in my head: cheese, chicken, buttered mushrooms, caramelised onions…it's missing something – another texture or another flavour.

Pan back on the heat…I saw pine nuts in the Black Box…with a bit of salt, toasted pine nuts will be the ingredient that lifts this pizza.

The final ingredient that gives this pizza a special flavour is smoked mozzarella.

A few days before I was in Beverly Hills at a cheese shop (most people are in LA star spotting and I'm in a cheese shop – I know, I've got to get a life) and that is where I tried smoked mozzarella for the first time. The flavour was so subtle but just lingered, it was beautiful and now I have an opportunity to use it on a pizza. It was a bit scary as I had never used it before and so I had no idea how it would cook on the pizza. It could have been a disaster – lucky for me it wasn't.

With all my toppings ready, I had about 20 minutes before I had to present to the judges and with ten minutes cooking time that gave me ten minutes to clean up my station and get organised.

With only one base allowed in the final, you cannot afford to make a mistake; there is no backup plan. I started to put my pizza together and then placed it into the oven. As I take it out, I notice it does need a few more minutes, so I put it back in and wait three more minutes. The competitor before me has finished, so it's my turn. Perfect. I take it back to my prep area and cut it into eight pieces, then decorate it with the toasted pine nuts and shave some parmesan cheese over it for that sharp bity taste. The few short steps to the judges table feels like forever… you don't want to trip and drop your pizza at this stage! As I place the pizza in front of the judges, I start to explain what flavours are on the pizza and as I'm talking I begin to smell the pizza as well: it looks great and it smells great. I feel it is the best pizza I could have made with the ingredients that were available. I'm happy.

Sean Brauser, chief coordinator of the Pizza Today competition, starts the award ceremony by asking the final four to line up in front of the audience. Then he calls out the winner of the traditional pizza, it's Eddy. Wow! It's her first time in the competition and she has won, that's great. She works for Graziano, one of Italy's greatest traditional pizza makers and, if this is her first time in the competition, imagine how good she will get the more she competes.

Then Sean continues: 'The winner of the best non-traditional pizza is…' then he breaks into how, in non-traditional, you can do whatever you want and that he saw some amazing pizzas over the three-day competition but none more different than this one. He looks at me and says, 'The winner of the best non-traditional pizza is Theo Kalogeracos'. I can't believe it, a dessert pizza has won, my dessert pizza, never before has a desert pizza even been entered let alone won. Unbelievable. Jackie (Sean's fiancé) hands me the trophy. I'm that excited that I give her the biggest hug. Wow that was something!

I go back in the line and Sean says: 'And now the final and the biggest award, 2010 Pizza Maker of the Year, is also the winner of the Black Box competition, and the winner is…' he calls out my name! I can't believe it, I'm speechless. You know how on some days when you think everything is working out okay? I just had one of those days.

I will never forget this day as it was the first time Liz was in Vegas with me (my lucky charm). It was great having her there, as everything we have, we have created together.

Black box

CARAMELISED ONIONS

a little olive oil
1 onion
salt
pepper
1 teaspoon brown sugar

COOKED MUSHROOMS

40 g mushrooms, chopped
1 tablespoon butter
1 tablespoon parsley, finely chopped

PIZZA

1 basic dough ball – rolled, rested & ready
90 g mozzarella, grated
50 g diced chicken
1 tablespoon cream
1 tablespoon pesto (p99)
caramelised onions
cooked mushrooms
40 g smoked mozzarella (you can smoke it yourself in your wood-fired oven, otherwise use any smoked cheese except for cheddar)

a handful of toasted pine nuts with salt
parmesan cheese (for shaving)

Pre-heat oven to 220°C

1. Place the onion into a pan with a little olive oil, salt and pepper and let it cook over a low heat until it has a nice light-brown colour.
2. Add the brown sugar and toss gently mix and the onion will begin to caramelise.
3. Set aside. It will caramelise fully as it cooks on the pizza.

1. Melt the butter in a pan and add the mushrooms, season to taste.
2. Cook the mushrooms for a few minutes, then remove from heat and toss through the parsley.
3. Set aside until it is time to add them to your pizza.

1. Mix the chicken, cream and pesto together in a bowl and leave to marinate.
2. Now is the time to caramelise the onions and cook the mushrooms.
3. To make the pizza, spread the grated mozzarella on the base then add the mushrooms, chicken and caramelised onions and finish with smoked mozzarella.
4. Cook for 7 to 10 minutes.
5. Sprinkle with toasted pine nuts and shaved parmesan.

JUDGING THE 2011 WORLD PIZZA CHAMPIONSHIP

Judging a pizza competition is a joy and a source of frustration all at the same time. It is so exciting to see what the next pizza chef is going to present to you, especially when it's done well, like my friend John Gutekanst from Athens, Ohio who made a roast suckling pig *scachatta* (it's a Sicilian-style pizza) that he finished off with Sardinian honey – absolutely amazing. Or Monica from Australia, her pizza with Bresaola, crème fraîche, watercress and an ingredient that I've always wanted to use, but never have: roasted beetroot. Monica inspired me to finally put beetroot on a pizza.

It was great to see Luigi from Italy making a non-traditional pizza with some new techniques. He had a smoked salmon pizza and this is the clever part, what we thought was some kind of salmon roe was actually reduced balsamic vinegar, put on the pizza with an eye dropper. He placed these little balls of balsamic vinegar all around the pizza so when you took a bite they would pop in your mouth. Very clever.

The frustrating part is sitting there judging when you would rather be on the other side of the table making the pizzas, that's what we all love to do. Sometimes you win and sometimes you lose, but you always walk away a better pizza chef than when you started.

I walked away from judging with a new pizza inspired by ideas from John (thanks mate, I'll buy you a beer next time Bruno is getting us lost in a van in Sallsa), Monica, her twin sister and Luigi. John provided the pork belly, Monica and her sister (thanks, you girls rock) the beetroot and Luigi his clever eye-dropper technique (grazie mille).

Remember, you always eat with your eyes first, so put as much effort into making your pizza look good as you put into making it taste good.

OLD SCHOOL VEGAS STYLE: CIRCO BELLAGIO HOTEL

Sirio Maccioni and his wife are Tuscan natives who travelled and cooked their way through Europe before settling in New York and opening their first restaurant in 1974 at the Mayfair hotel, Le Cirque. His reputation grew and the restaurant became renowned, it even won the James Beard award for restaurant of the year in 1995. When Sirio and his family were asked to set up a restaurant in Las Vegas,

2 ROAD TRIP *Las Vegas*

everybody expected something great, and they delivered. But for me, what I didn't expect was to find such a fine dining establishment serving the humble pizza, and a real traditional pizza at that: there are no bells and whistles with their pizza, it is simply one of the best traditional pizzas you are going to find anywhere.

If you find yourself having a meal at Circo in Vegas, don't just order pizza because all the food there is outstanding. But you should try to order at least one pizza for the table to start your meal. We ordered two: one with mushrooms, fontina cheese and ricotta – these are very simple and great flavours, you get the earthiness of the mushrooms and the nice flavour that the fontina gives along with a creaminess that only ricotta can give – and one with spinach, ricotta and truffle oil. This was another great pizza following the less-is-more rule: two main ingredients being showcased and not fighting for your attention among a heap of other ingredients.

All the pizzas are baked in an old school brick oven, that looks like it was pulled out of an early-1900s pizzeria in New York and shipped to Vegas one brick at a time. Well, if they did go to all that trouble for the oven, it was worth it, and you will know it when you take your first bite. It was one of the best crispy bases I've had on a pizza. It's bizarre to be sitting in a fancy restaurant in the Bellagio Hotel in the middle of Las Vegas eating a pizza that could have been made by a Nonna in a small village in the hills of Tuscany. That's what the pizza at Circo does for you: it shows you the Maccioni family roots and it shows you that pizza can also be a serious food holding its own next to every dish on a fine-dining menu.

Wood-fired pork loin with balsamic tears

WOOD-FIRED PORK LOIN

- 2 kg pork loin (get your butcher to score the skin for you and ask for some belly to be left on it)
- 1 tablespoon salt
- 1 teaspoon cracked black pepper
- 1 teaspoon cracked fennel seeds
- 1 teaspoon cracked mustard seeds
- olive oil

PIZZA

- 1 basic pizza dough ball – rolled, rested & ready
- 90 g mozzarella, grated
- 110 g wood-fired pork loin, sliced
- 40 g roasted beetroot wedges (p99)

- 1 tablespoon balsamic glaze for 'tears'
- 2 tablespoons of horseradish cream
- 1 tablespoon micro basil with flowers (or normal fresh basil leaves)

Pre-heat oven to 220°C

1. Place the pork loin uncovered in the fridge for a minimum of 12 hours – this will help you get really crispy crackling.
2. When you are ready to roast your pork, place it on your bench, drizzle the meat (not the skin) with olive oil, rub in the salt, pepper, fennel and mustard seeds then roll it up. If you can tie it with string, do so; if not, roll it as tight as you can then place it in a tray with a V-rack. By using a pan with a rack you get a rotisserie-style cooking with heat flowing under and over the pork cooking it evenly and allowing the smoke from the wood in your oven to give the pork a really unique flavour.
3. Cook at 200°C for 60 to 80 minutes. If you have a meat thermometer you want it to read 60°C for perfectly oven-roasted pork loin.

1. Sprinkle mozzarella evenly over the base, then place the roasted pork loin and beetroot wedges around the pizza; try not to put any beetroot in the middle as they are heavy and will slide off the pizza slices.
2. Cook for 7 to 10 minutes.
3. When ready, cut into eight pieces, dollop horseradish onto each slice, then place the basil onto the horseradish, then carefully place small droplets of balsamic glaze around the pizza. Serve immediately!

NEW YORK
A GOOD PIZZA SLICE IS HARD TO FIND

New York. There are some things that you have to do when you go there, like have a hot dog on the street out of a push cart; visit the Statue of Liberty; go to the top of the Empire State Building; have a smoked salmon bagel at Murray's; and also, a must, is the New York pizza slice. And boy, are you going to be disappointed. The majority of pizza slices sold in New York are rubbish, just made to feed the masses. It takes as much time to make a bad pizza as it does to make a great pizza – have all these guys lost their zest to make great pizza? Do they think they are doing New York's reputation a favour? No, please stop. A great New York pizza slice is a thing of beauty, as big as your own head, you have to fold it down the middle just so your mouth can have a chance of taking a bite. As you start to chew the light and fluffy base, you get hit with that great pizza sauce that nobody makes like a true New Yorker – using San Marzano tomatoes. Then there is the cheese – what can I say? it's real mozzarella cheese, not the oil slick you find on a bad NY pizza slice. It's cooked to perfection, nice and creamy and with a hint of flavour. It's those three things that make a great New York slice. Good luck in finding it.

LOMBARDI'S

The first pizzeria to open in America was Lombardi's, in 1905, run by Gennaro Lombardi. It operated from the same location until 1984 when the doors closed forever.

In 1994 Gennaro Lombardi III and his friend John Brescio went to the original location and found the original face of the coal oven, took it with them and opened up the new-but-old Lombardi's just a block away.

The minute I walked in I loved the place: cash only, red and white chequered tablecloths, dark wood everywhere, slow-moving ceiling fans, photos of famous celebrities. But the best bit is when you walk in and your nose starts working overtime; the place has a really nice aroma – tomato sauce, oregano, cheese being melted: it smells like the real deal.

I'm about to eat at America's first pizzeria and from the menu, one pizza jumps straight out at me:

Clam pie (no sauce), 14", $26
More than 2 dozen hand shucked clams, oregano, garlic-infused oil, grated pecorino, Romano cheese, virgin olive oil, black pepper, topped with fresh parsley and served with fresh lemon.

I'm sold, that's the pizza for me.

As I'm waiting for my pizza to be made, I watch the pizzas going to other tables and they all look good. I am hoping I made a good choice, as I don't see any clam pizzas going to tables.

My pizza arrives and it looks simple enough – the clams smell like they were freshly shucked and cooked just for my pizza; and there are a ton of them. I pick up a slice and notice a nice, slightly charred base from the coal oven. I take my first bite, and its good, oh yeah, it's really good: it has that nice brick-oven crunch but is soft and chewy in the middle, and as there is no sauce which makes it light. My first thought is there is no way I'm going to eat a 14 inch pizza on my own, but after the first couple of bites I'm glad I don't have to share it.

The combination of clams with oregano, pecorino and Romano cheese with the hint of black pepper and lemon squeezed on top was simply bliss, so I tried to recreate it when I got home. After many failed attempts I think this is as close as I can get to Lombardi's without having to fly back to New York.

New York pizza dough

700 ml cold tap water
70 ml olive oil
1.4 kg strong bakers flour
20 g yeast
1 tablespoon salt
1 teaspoon sugar
extra flour for dusting
semolina for pizza peel

Makes five 14 inch New York pizzas

1. Pour the water and the olive oil into the mixing bowl first (this will help the dry ingredients distribute evenly) then add the flour, yeast, salt, and sugar. Mix on low speed for seven minutes, then check the dough by feeling it, it should be soft bordering on tacky (New York dough is softer than most other types of dough). Mix for another seven minutes on low speed, take the dough out of the machine and place it on a bench dusted with extra flour and mould the dough to form one big smooth ball. Place this in a sealed container that is double the size of the dough as it will need room to grow, and leave in the fridge for a minimum of 10 hours and a maximum of 24 hours.
2. Bring the dough back to room temperature for an hour before using it; if it is still cold in the middle it will be difficult to stretch.
3. Take your dough out of the container and place it on the bench. It should be slightly tacky but not sticking to your hands. If it is too soft and tacky, add some extra flour so you can work it. Divide it into five even pieces – each should weigh around 400 g.
4. A New York pizza chef never uses a rolling pin and they do not mould up a tight dough ball. Instead, they take their piece of dough, roll it in flour and use the palm of their hand to start pushing and stretching the dough to get it to the size they want. A New York pizza is not perfectly round and it should have extra bubbles in it from the 10-hour fermentation process. You notice air bubbles in your dough, don't pop them but leave them there; they will add a great crunchy texture to the crust when it is baked.
5. Place the stretched dough on a pizza peel that is lightly dusted with fine semolina – this will help you slide the pizza into the oven later – and let it rest for 10 minutes before you add the toppings.

New York-style clam

CLAMS

2 dozen (approximately a kilo) fresh-frozen clams (use fresh when in season)
1 cup of white wine
2 teaspoons of dried or fresh oregano
2 large cloves of garlic, finely chopped
pinch of black pepper
pinch of sea salt
extra virigin olive oil

PIZZA

1 dough ball, New York pizza style
50 g mozzarella, grated
30 g pecorino, grated
30 g romano, grated
1 kg cooked clams

1 teaspoon parsley, freshly chopped
extra virgin olive oil to drizzle
1 lemon, cut into wedges

---

1. Rinse your clams under cold running water and then let them drain in a colander. Get a pot large enough to fit your clams and put it on a medium heat. Place your clams in the pot with the wine (the rule with wine is: if you can't drink it, don't cook with it). Cover and steam for five minutes. Check to see if all the clams have opened. If not, put the lid back on and continue to steam for another two minutes.

2. Take the pot off the heat, pour the clams into a colander and drain the liquid. Throw away any unopened clams as they're no good.

3. Let the clams cool down before removing the meat from the shells. Leave eight intact for decorating the pizza.

4. In a bowl place all of the clam meat and the eight whole clam shells, then add oregano, garlic, salt, pepper and a drizzle of extra virgin olive oil and mix together. Then it is ready to go on your pizza.

Pre-heat oven to 250°C

1. Sprinkle the mozzarella, pecorino and romano evenly on the pizza base making sure that you stop just before the edge so the pizza has a crust all the way round.

2. Spread the clam meat and its marinade over the pizza, decorate with the eight whole shells, and slide it gently into the oven.

3. Cook for 5 to 7 minutes. The clams are already cooked so you have to be careful not to overcook the pizza. You are after a nice golden crust with the cheese bubbling away, then it is ready to come out. Using the peel, have a look under the crust to check that you have that nice golden color.

4. When ready, pull the pizza out and slide it onto a cutting board, then cut it and sprinkle over the parsley followed by a drizzle of extra virgin olive oil. Then place the lemon wedges on the pizza and serve.

5. Make sure you squeeze the lemon onto your slice of pizza, then, as you take the first bite, the lemon will be the first thing you taste then the sweet taste of the clam, and as you bite into the dough you will find that New York dough is like no other, is has a real crunch to it with a chewy middle that is addictive when it is done well.

MY NEW YORK MOMENTS

Realising university was not for me, I left school as soon as I could and became a baker: one of the hardest jobs ever. I've always had a good work ethic and I've always been able to work 18-hour shifts day after day and survive on four or five hours sleep, in fact, nothing's changed in twenty years or so, I still do the same number of hours. They say that when you are born a donkey, you die a donkey.

This donkey never read books at school, had no other interest except cars, rock and roll, work, and girls, in that order. It was not until the year 2000 that I read my first book from cover to cover, unable to put it down. It blew my mind. I was reading a book that spoke to me; it felt like I was the main character. You have to understand, this had never happened to me before and here I was, absolutely loving a book. It wasn't a fictional book and it wasn't a book that was turned into a movie. No, it was the book that told me it was okay to be working when everybody else goes out, that it's alright never to have a Friday, Saturday or Sunday off. This book, as it says on the cover, is about adventures in the culinary underbelly: *Kitchen Confidential*, by Anthony Bourdain.

The first time I went to New York, there was only one place I wanted to go to eat and that was where Bourdain worked, at Les Halles. And guess who is sitting at the bar? Yep, there he was. I felt like a stalker. I had to talk to him, get him to sign my book and a photo, he was so cool.

Now that I like reading, I'm his greatest fan and I've got all his books: *Medium Raw, No Reservations, Gone Bamboo, Bone in the Throat, Typhoid Mary, The Nasty Bits, A Cook's Tour, Bobby Gold, Les Halles the Cookbook*.

Just as *Kitchen Confidential* spoke to me like no other book, there is one movie that captures the real chaos of a busy restaurant (we call it controlled chaos) and I've watched it hundreds of times. It shows a real kitchen with all the good elements and all the bad, the dodgy staff, food critics, loyal customers, annoying customers, losing power in the middle of a Saturday night – this still happens all the time. This movie was directed by Bob Giraldi who also owns restaurants in New York and I think that is why it is so good. The movie is *Dinner Rush*, starring Danny Aiello and Edoardo Ballerini. Danny owns a restaurant in the trendy Tribeca area of New York called Gigino's, and that is where the whole movie is filmed.

So a few years have passed since I met Anthony Bourdain and I find myself back in New

York. My first dinner is at Gigino's. Bob Giraldi, the director of the movie, still owns it and apart from it looking a lot bigger in the movie, it is exactly the same. It is a lovely Italian trattoria. I sit at the bar and I am feeling like I'm an extra in the movie, and I order a nice glass of Chianti, pizza for starters then a bowl of pasta, dessert and then I'll be ready for bed.

The pizza I ordered was called Tribeca, and was topped with spinach, chicken, bacon and scamorza cheese. It was cooked to perfection in a wood-fired oven, the base was made with New York style dough, and it had a beautiful aroma with a nice creaminess coming from the cheese.

For my pasta dish I ordered Gigino's signature dish: beetroot pasta with julienne beets, escarole hearts, garlic olive oil, and crispy colatura-flavoured crumbs. This pasta dish looked spectacular. At Gigino's they make their own fresh pasta with beetroot in the dough, so you end up with deep red pasta – visually one of the best pasta dishes I've seen and the flavours and textures did not let it down. I ordered some crusty bread and another glass of red and finished the lot.

NEW YORK UPSIDE-DOWN PIZZA

This pizza is one of the better pizza slices (it is cut into squares) you will find walking around NY. It's a great, simple pizza with only dough, sauce and cheese and kids absolutely love it.

You will find that this pizza is made in extra-large baking trays like those bakers use; the dough is similar to the teglia dough used in Italy. The reason it is called an upside-down pizza is because of the order of the toppings where the sauce is put on top of the mozzarella.

The following recipe will make 800 g dough. If you have a large baking tray, roll it all out till it covers your tray, or just make it fit whatever size tray you have. Remember it is a thick base. I use 400 g to fit a 34 cm x 24 cm tray.

BLONDIE PIZZA

Blondie the band started out in New York in the '70s at CBGB's in Manhattan. Blondie the dessert pizza is as delicious as Debbie Harry and is inspired by a white brownie I tried at Amy's Breads at the Chelsea Market in New York. The recipe is not that hard, the one thing that you have to do is cook it like a brownie so it has a chewy center, not like a cake fully cooked and spongy.

Honeycomb. You can buy it everywhere, but you probably don't realise how easy it is to make. The Blondie pizza has honeycomb in it and if you don't have time, buying good honeycomb is easy…but if you try the honeycomb recipe for this pizza you will have leftover to eat on its own, the recipe only needs 70 g.

Tribeca

Tribeca in Lower Manhattan is a vibrant neighbourhood buzzing with creative people rubbing shoulders with the wealthy. It is becoming famous for the Tribeca Film Festival founded by Robert de Niro, and many movies and sit-coms are filmed there. It is also the home of Gigino's – the real star of the movie, *Dinner Rush*.

1 New York pizza dough ball
 – rested, stretched & ready
100 g scamorza (or provolone), grated
1 cup baby spinach leaves, washed, dried and sprinkled with pinch of salt and pepper
100 g roasted chicken, shredded
100 g smoked, uncooked bacon, diced

Pre-heat oven to 275°C

1. Place the baby spinach leaves on your prepared dough, then top evenly with scamorza cheese.

2. Add the roasted chicken and smoked bacon, and sprinkle a pinch of salt.

3. Cook for 5 to 7 minutes, then cut it up and serve.

New York upside-down

UPSIDE-DOWN PIZZA DOUGH

- 500 g strong bakers flour
- 15 g fresh yeast
- 240 ml luke-warm water
- 2 tablespoons extra virgin olive oil
- 10 g salt
- 4 tablespoons semolina

UPSIDE-DOWN TOMATO SAUCE

- 400 g tin whole peeled tomatoes
- 20 ml olive oil
- $\frac{1}{2}$ teaspoon oregano
- $\frac{1}{4}$ teaspoon salt
- pinch of sugar
- 1 clove of garlic, finely chopped

PIZZA

- 1 ball upside-down pizza dough – rested, stretched and ready
- 500 g mozzarella, thinly sliced
- 2 cups of upside-down tomato sauce
- $\frac{1}{2}$ cup of romano cheese, grated

Pre-heat oven to 220°C

1. Add yeast to water, whisk and leave to sit for five minutes.
2. Add flour, salt and oil to the water and yeast and mix for ten minutes.
3. Cut the dough into two even pieces, rub with oil to cover and rest for 15 minutes under a tea towel.
4. Grease your tray with oil.
5. On the bench, spread out two tablespoons of semolina then place the dough on top and spread it out using your hands to the size of your tin. Then place flattened dough into tin. Placing semolina on the bench first will result in a crunchy base when the pizza is cooked.
6. Let the dough rest for 30 minutes before adding toppings.

1. Place all the ingredients in a deep bowl and start breaking up the tomatoes using a potato masher. The reason you use a masher is so you don't blend the tomatoes into a sauce; you want to see pieces of tomato on your upside-down pizza.

1. Place the sliced mozzarella on the base and then spread the tomato sauce evenly around, covering the mozzarella.
2. Sprinkle the romano cheese over and cook 15 minutes.
3. Leave to cool for 5 minutes before cutting up into squares, and serve each slice on greaseproof paper.

Blondie

HONEYCOMB

80 g (4 tablespoons) golden syrup
200 g caster sugar
3 teaspoons bicarb soda, sieved

WHITE BROWNIE MIX

80 g melted butter
140 g brown or caster sugar
1 egg
1 teaspoon vanilla paste
pinch of salt
140 g self-raising flour
70 g broken honeycomb

PIZZA

2 basic pizza dough balls
 – rolled, rested & ready
1 portion of white brownie mix

icing sugar for dusting
double cream
extra honeycomb

Pre-heat oven to 220°C

1. Line a 20 x 20 cm baking tray with grease-proof paper.
2. Pour the golden syrup into a small saucepan and add the sugar on top. Let the sugars dissolve over medium heat, do not stir. After three minutes, stir for two minutes until all the sugar has dissolved, then turn the heat down low and simmer for 5 minutes – do not stir.
3. Add the bicarb soda and stir for 30 seconds over low heat, making sure all the bicarb is incorporated into the sugar mix – it will start to rise and puff up. Remove from heat after 30 seconds and pour into the prepared tin.
4. Leave to cool for a minimum of 20 minutes before eating or using.

1. In a mixing bowl whisk melted butter and sugar till light and fluffy, about 3 minutes.
2. Add egg and vanilla and mix on slow for a minute.
3. Add salt and flour, mix on low speed for 1 minute and then on medium speed for 1 minute. Gently fold in the broken honeycomb.

1. Spread the white brownie mix evenly over the pizza base.
2. Cook 5 to 7 minutes.
3. When ready, pull the pizza out, cut into 8 slices and sprinkle over the icing sugar. Then top with a dollop of cream with a piece of honeycomb on each slice to serve.

SAN FRANCISCO
FOLLOW THE CROWDS TO FIND THE BEST FOOD

The first day I arrive in a new city, I get up around 6.30 am, have a shower, get dressed, get my notepad and start walking. I follow the masses because that's when you see where they stop for coffee or a pastry. It's a great way to find out where the locals go and to get a feel for the city.

Liz and I arrived in San Francisco on a Friday night, so Saturday morning I was off. We were staying at the Fisherman's Wharf, which is a great area to be based in when you are in San Fran.

As I followed the water towards the Golden Gate Bridge I started to notice more and more people heading in the same direction I was walking and then I walked straight into one of the best food markets ever, the Fisherman's Wharf markets that are only open on Saturdays. I know, how lucky was I? There was everything there from fresh fruit and vegetables to honey, seafood, kitchen shops, book stores, sliced cured meats, everything. But the best was a stall selling slow-cooked roast pork belly in a sourdough roll with onions cooked in white wine. They only have one thing for sale, that's it, nothing fancy. Crusty bread stuffed with pork meat and crackling then a beautiful arrangement of onions cooked in white wine, sensational.

I walked back to the hotel, got Liz out of bed and took her to the markets. She wanted a coffee to wake up and I said forget it, get the pork roll first before they run out. We ordered two and sat on a bench looking at the bridge eating our rolls – it doesn't get better than this. Actually, if Chaz was with us then it couldn't get any better.

TONY'S PIZZA NAPOLETANA

I went looking for one of the true pioneers Californian-style pizza and also an inspiring leader, teaching Americans to eat seasonal produce, shop locally, and live sustainably: Alice Waters.

As you drive down Shattuck Ave in Berkeley, California you start to feel the gravity of the area. There are young, beautiful people sitting on the grass in the median strip catching some sun having a pastry. I can see a lot of pizza boxes being carried around. You also see the mature, beautiful people walking around, checking out the eclectic shops that line the road, or find that local café bursting at the seams with the lunch crowd.

Maybe it has been done on purpose but it feels like Chez Panisse is stuck in the '80s, which is not a bad thing, the pizzas were great. It just felt that outside there was something exciting happening, and inside was a time warp.

And outside I did find something exciting, Tony's Pizza Napoletana.

Don't let the name fool you; this is no run-of-the-mill pizza store. Tony's is the best pizza experience you will have; it may be the best pizzeria in all of America at the moment. The brain-child of three passionate people, Nancy, Bruno and, as the sign says, Tony.

It's a pizza lover's paradise, you could write a whole book just on what they do, so let's get some figures straight: they use four different ovens (NY-style flat top, gas brick oven, domed gas oven, and a wood-fired oven), four different types of flour (5 Stagioni, Pendleton, Caputo, and San Felice) and make seven different styles of pizza: STG Napoletana, Classic Italian, Classic American, Stromboli, Sicilian, Calzone and Romana.

A logistical nightmare but somehow it works well. I must have put on at least 3 kg from eating at Tony's – we went there for dinner and ate so much I rolled back to Fisherman's Wharf. But it was that good that I went back the next night to try the pizzas that I didn't have the first time, so I'm going to give you a rundown of what I ate:

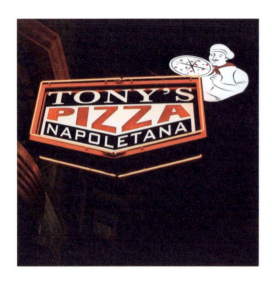

Pizza Romana – this pizza is served on a long wooden board with a stand lifting it off the table; there are three different sensations on one pizza: salty, sweet, and sour. On one side of the pizza there are cherry tomatoes, black olives, basil and garlic; in the middle there is salami picante, rocket, parmesan; and at the other end sweet fig preserve, prosciutto and gorgonzola. With all this on one pizza I didn't need to order another one. But I had to try more.

Classic Italian – this pizza is cooked in a domed gas oven. It has vine-ripened tomato sauce, it is hand tossed and the base is made from 5 Stagioni flour.

Cal Italian – asiago, mozzarella, gorgonzola, sweet fig, prosciutto di parma, parmesan and balsamic reduction.

Classic American – the original Tomato Pie, baked in a New York–style flat top gas brick oven with hand crushed tomato sauce, hand tossed dough using Pendleton flour.

New Jersey–style – slices of mozzarella, tomato sauce, oregano, garlic, parmesan and olive oil. I took one look at this pizza when it came to the table, and I said to myself: I'm not going to like this pizza. The base was thick, the sauce was on top it's not the kind of pizza I would order but it ended up being one of my favourites. It's got no fancy ingredients on it, but the sauce on that light crunchy base, wow it blew me away. The flavours jumped at me – the original tomato pie from New Jersey gets the thumbs up.

Calzone – the deep-fried, Brooklyn-style calzone was sensational – covered with mozzarella, garlic, spinach and ricotta. Order this one for the table as a starter.

Rustic Scorola con Pancetta – this is a pizza that I would fly all the way from Australia to San Francisco just to eat it again. The dough is made from Caputo flour with an irresistible combination of crushed red peppers, mozzarella, pancetta, peppered goat's cheese, escarole (endive) and sweet piquante peppers. A true masterpiece of flavours and textures.

New Haven–style, thin crust with clam and garlic – clams, mozzarella, oregano, garlic and parmesan. No tinned clams used on this pizza: the first bit you have will verify that these are freshly shucked clams.

Rustic, medium crust with truffle – mozzarella burrata, Cowgirl Creamery Mt. Tam triple cream cheese, wild mushrooms, rocket, parmesan and shaved truffle. This pizza is seasonal and the truffles are flown in from Italy. Tony's buys about 4 oz of truffles per week, so when it is truffle season make sure you order this pizza as you are going to have to wait another year if you miss it.

Rustic, medium crust with quail egg and speck – this pizza base is made from Caputo flour with mozzarella, quail eggs, smoked Italian speck, rocket and fontina cheese. The pizza is cooked without the eggs and when it's got about two minutes to go they take it out of the oven and then crack the eggs onto the toppings, return it to the oven to finish it off and slightly cook the eggs. When it's served the eggs have that slight runny yolk mixing with the speck, beautiful.

Rum-marinated bananas with cinnamon and toasted coconut – Tony's dessert pizza breaks the dessert pizza rules as it has mozzarella cheese on it, but it is ever so slight that you don't even notice it; its main job is to hold all the beautiful ingredients together.

STG Napoletana, Margherita – you have to be approved by the Italian pizza police to be able to make this pizza, not just anybody can call their pizza STG Margherita, there are rules. You have to cook it in a 900°F (480°C) wood-fired oven, the dough has to be mixed by hand using San Felice flour, then left to prove in wooden boxes that come from Naples, the tomatoes in the sauce have to be San Marzano DOP, you are only allowed to add sea salt to the sauce and it has to be kept at room temperature, the mozzarella you use has to be Fior di Latte, fresh basil must be used, and the pizza has to cook in 90 seconds.

So if you find yourself in San Francisco and you get a seat at Tony's and you want to order one of these amazing Margheritas, you'd better get your order in quick as they only make 73 each day and once they run out, they run out.

A NEW PIZZA

When I returned home I started to cook pork belly to try and get that same flavour I remembered from the markets at Fisherman's Wharf in San Fran and I think it's close. Then I thought, if I can make a sourdough pizza base and put the pork with the onions on a pizza, well then I've come up with a killer pizza, and here it is. It is a time-consuming pizza as good sourdough needs at least 24 hours to make and to slow cook the pork you are looking at 2 to 3 hours, so what I think you should do is cook the pork and have it for dinner one night and then the next day use the leftovers to make the pizza.

The sour part in sourdough is called biga, which is a starter, a natural fermentation to aerate your dough and give it a distinctive flavour. Back in the day before yeast was readily available, people used grapes, apples, potatoes anything that would ferment to make a natural starter. You can replace the yeast in the biga with one of those if you like, but I will give you a fool-proof recipe and then you can muck around with it.

2 ROAD TRIP *San Francisco*

San Fran sourdough pizza base

This recipe will give you 1.3 kg of dough, which is enough for five pizzas.

BIGA

440 g bakers flour
500 ml tap water
5 g (1 teaspoon) instant dry yeast

SOURDOUGH

500 g bakers flour
8 g (1½ teaspoons) salt
50 ml water
biga

1. Place all ingredients in an extra-large bowl (it needs to be big enough for the biga to triple in size).

2. Whisk together until the yeast has dissolved and all the flour has been incorporated into the water.

3. Cover the bowl with cling wrap and place in the fridge. The biga can be used after 3 hours but for a stronger sourdough fermentation flavour, leave it for 24 hours.

1. Place water, then the biga, followed by flour and salt in a mixing bowl and bring together using a dough hook on low speed for 3 minutes.

2. Check: is it too firm? Does it need some water? Is it too soft? Does it need more flour? Adjust and mix for a further 7 minutes – the dough should be firm but slightly tacky.

3. Remove dough hook and cover the dough in the mixing bowl with cling wrap. Leave for 2 to 3 hours until the dough has doubled in size.

4. Remove the dough and cut into 5 even pieces, about 260 g per dough ball for a 12 inch pizza. Flatten the dough, sprinkle with flour and roll out to the size of the tray. Leave on tray for 30 minutes to 1 hour until the dough has doubled in size.

Slow-cooked pork belly & white wine onions on sourdough

SLOW-COOKED PORK BELLY

1 kg pork belly (ask your butcher to score the skin for you)
½ teaspoon rock salt
½ teaspoon black peppercorns
1 tablespoon fennel seeds
4 large white onions, peeled and quartered
3 large cloves of garlic, peeled
olive oil
1 bottle white wine – ½ for cooking, ½ for drinking with your pizza

Pre-heat oven to its highest temperature, fan off

1. In a mortar place the salt, pepper and fennel and crush up to a nice smooth powder. Rub into pork belly skin, especially the score marks.

2. Place the onions and garlic in a heavy oven-proof dish and drizzle with a good amount of oil. Place the pork belly on top and put in the oven for 10 minutes. This will help the skin to become crispy, which will give you great crackling. After 10 minutes turn the temperature down to 170°C and roast for 1 hour.

3. Pour ½ a bottle of white wine into the dish. It needs another hour but check after 30 minutes and if all the wine has evaporated add some water – you want to keep the onions moist so they don't start to burn and go black. You will know your pork belly is ready when you have a golden colored crackle and the meat looks like it will melt in your mouth. Serves four people or makes three 12 inch pizzas.

4. If you are cooking this pork just for pizza you need to let the meat rest for 10 minutes before you cut it up. If using leftovers, take the pork and onions out of the fridge and bring to room temperature.

PIZZA

1 x 12 inch sourdough pizza base – rolled and proofed
90 g mozzarella, grated
140 g diced roast pork belly
3 tablespoons white wine onions

Pre-heat oven to 250°C

1. This pizza has no sauce, it doesn't need it. The meat is really moist and the onions are full of wine so there is enough moisture and flavour on the pizza already.

2. Spread mozzarella on the pizza base with more at the outer edges than in the centre. Place the diced pork belly evenly around pizza and cover the pork with the onion mixture.

3. Cook for 7 to 10 minutes.

4. Don't worry about adding any garnish or anything fancy when you serve this pizza. Just sit back, enjoy the crusty sourdough base and the slow-roasted pork belly with white wine oven-roasted onions flavour combination that you will never forget.

LOS ANGELES
DO IT WITH LOVE AND PLAY IT LOUD

When you think LA, the first thing you think is Hollywood and you would be right: all the iconic places and the Hollywood sign are everywhere as you drive around – but good pizza is not. I have been lucky enough to go to LA many times for work, so much so that I now drive myself around and I made it my mission to find great pizza in LA, but at first it was a desert, nothing great at all.

SPAGOS

My journey started at Spagos. Like Alice Waters in San Francisco, Wolfgang Puck is credited with starting the revolution of Californian-style pizza which means fresh ingredients, innovation and experimentation. He did this with the help of Ed LaDou, who created the menu for a big pizza chain called California Pizza Kitchen. But, like Alice Waters in San Fran, this part of LA is stuck in a time warp. All of the places I ate at were good but would I go back? Hell no. I've found the future of pizza in LA, you can call it whatever style you want; I call it great. So let's leave the glitz of Hollywood and the bright lights behind and head out to the suburbs.

PITFIRE ARTISAN PIZZA

As I walk in the first thing I see on the wall is Daniel Johnston's 'Hi, how are you' mural (they did a doco on him, *The Devil and Daniel Johnston*). The music is up too loud, I love that too (play what you want, as loud as you want and if they don't like it tell them to go to the golden arches for some muzak) but these are only signs of being cool. The real test is their pizza, and boy can they make a pizza, one of the best crusts in LA.

David and Paul from Pitfire don't even consider themselves part of the pizza industry; all their pizzerias are in the 'burbs, the food is real food for real people and the lines tell you that they are onto a good thing and sticking to it. The one comment I keep hearing from David is 'I would not be doing what I'm doing if I didn't think it's outstanding pizza'.

It would be hard to top a pizza from Pitfire. I'll give you a run-down of what we ate and you will be licking your lips by the time you finish reading. Luckily I was with friends so we could order heaps and I could try everything. We had:

Farmers Market Roasted Vegetables – which come with whipped ricotta and grilled bread.

Hand Chopped Salad – made with crunchy lettuce, garbanzo beans, cannellini beans, tomatoes, red onion, mozzarella and roasted corn. For me a fresh salad with pizza is like peaches and cream, perfect.

Organic Pumpkin Pie – organic pumpkin, toasted pepitas, wild greens, fontina cheese and pumpkin seed oil.

The Burrata Pie – burrata cheese, tomato sauce, wild rocket, caramelised onion, and a drizzle of hazelnut pesto.

Margherita – like I say, if they can't make a good Margherita, what's the point of trying anything else? Pitfire's Margherita is great!

Pitfire Sausage – a sweet fennel sausage with crushed tomato, fontina cheese, mozzarella and red onions.

I could go on and on, but I'm scared that David and Paul may think they have befriended a stalker. Thanks guys for the hospitality and outstanding pizza. (PS. and thanks for getting Liz and I so close to the sign…don't worry, your secret is safe with us).

MOZZA, WEST HOLLYWOOD

I've spent many days in LA on my own and there is one place I keep coming back to, where I can sit at the bar for one of my all-time favourite pizza crusts, and I don't feel alone. Maybe it's the über-cool setting, or that the bartender is great, or that the atmosphere is comforting with the wood-fired pizza oven going flat out in the background, whatever it is, I always feel at home at Mozza.

But all of the above doesn't count for anything if the food is no good; hands down Nancy Silverton's dough is the best. It's stretched to perfection by the pizzaolo and when it hits the bricks in the oven, the edges puff up to give you the most incredible crust. They use a special technique for stretching the dough at Mozza in order to get a crispy crust that is soft on the inside. The crust lip of the pizza is called cornicione, it may look easy but it's not – that's years of hard work making it look simple. So start drooling, for these are the pizzas we had:

Fennel Sausage – fennel sausage, cream, red onions and spring onions

Funghi Misti – mushrooms, fontina, taleggio and thyme

Speck – speck, buffalo mozzarella, olive tapenade and oregano

Pizzette – king trumpet mushrooms, ramp (wild leek), peas and pancetta

Egg & Bacon – egg, bacon, Yukon Gold potatoes and Bermuda onions

Bianca – fontina cheese, mozzarella, sottocenere (Italian truffle cheese) and sage

Gorgonzola – gorgonzola dolce, fingerling potatoes, radicchio and rosemary

We had a great dessert in the most unusual combination of olive oil ice-cream, it was smooth and rich. When I got home I started to experiment to come up with a recipe that came close to what I experienced and I hope you will give it a go. Before you do though, don't let anybody tell you it's easy to make ice-cream without an ice-cream maker, it's not. If you know how, that's great, but this recipe is for an ice-cream maker.

Easy olive oil ice-cream

A great extra virgin olive oil has a freshness to it, like you are standing in the middle of a field of grass, you can almost taste the grass in a great oil, its colour should have a slight green tinge to it, not yellow.

This recipe makes 1 litre – and remember: the better quality ingredients you use, the better the ice cream will be.

4 large egg yolks
150 g caster sugar
150 ml double cream
½ teaspoon vanilla paste
100 ml milk
150 ml extra virgin olive oil

extra olive oil to drizzle
sea salt

1. Slowly cream together your egg yolks and caster sugar, gradually increasing the speed to maximum for 2 minutes. Turn off, scrape bowl down and mix on high for another 3 minutes, scrape down again.

2. Pour in the double cream and mix for 1 minute until it's incorporated, scrape down and then mix for 3 minutes. You really want to whisk the cream on high till it is light and fluffy; this is the stage that will make sure you will get really smooth ice-cream.

3. Scrape down the bowl and place ½ teaspoon of vanilla paste into the cream then turn mixer on to low and slowly drizzle the milk in, mix for 3 minutes, turn off and scrape down.

4. Turn mixer on low and drizzle in your extra virgin olive oil and mix for 2 minutes.

5. Pour the mixture into your ice-cream maker and follow its instructions (my machine takes 27 minutes). You can serve the ice-cream straight from the ice-cream maker, but I like my olive oil ice cream to freeze for minimum of 3 hours before I serve it up.

6. Scoop the ice-cream into a bowl and drizzle over the tiniest amount of the same extra virgin olive oil and then sprinkle a small pinch of sea salt on top. I know what you are thinking, SALT but yes, salt. Salt is an enhancer that brings out the best in the ingredients you use and by putting this on top it will really bring out the flavours of the cream and the vanilla and especially the oil.

CECCONI'S

Thursday, 7.15 pm, Melrose Ave, West Hollywood, $90 White Truffle Pizza.

Have I got your attention?

When Ann & Joel from LASates.com asked me out to dinner, I had no idea I would be dining with all the glitterati of Hollywood and was about to eat the most expensive pizza that I've ever eaten.

Cecconi's is proud of its Italian background and so they should be. Everything we ordered was amazing, they stay true to what is real Italian cooking and eating.

I don't know how I got to be in LA in this restaurant with these new friends about to eat something that, even with the right planning, could go horribly wrong. But on this night the planets had all lined up and the gods were smiling upon us.

The white truffle season in Italy is so short that when it's missed, it's missed for a whole year. Sitting at the table watching the waitress shaving a fist-sized white truffle, flown in from the Alba region of Italy, onto our Bianco pizza was a sight to be seen. Bianco means white, and all that was on this pizza was some mild goat's cheese until the fine shavings of white truffle fell from the sky and hit it. The aroma coming from that pizza is something you don't forget. It was the first time I had eaten white truffle and the smell and taste were divine, very subtle earthy flavours that keep on surprising you with every bite. It was a pizza that I did not want to end.

After eating the pizza we were lucky to get a tour of the kitchen and this is where the secret lies: there was not one person in that kitchen who did not love their work, they all had real passion and the young pizzaolo who made our pizza was the real deal. He explained that they only use Italian flour, Italian cheeses and that he bakes all his pizzas in a brick oven with wood burning in the back making his pizzas truly artisan.

RED VELVET

Liz has a really sweet tooth. If it's got sugar or chocolate in it and it's good, Liz knows about it. When we were staying in LA for a few days she found this cupcake shop that she had seen on Oprah and she kept banging on to me about how amazing they were and there was me with my attitude that just because it's on TV doesn't make it good, so I didn't want to go.

But one early morning (Liz-early – 10.30) we walk to Sprinkles Cupcakes in Beverly Hills. It's a tiny shop with only two tables outside and a sign on the door telling you to close the door so the cupcakes don't dry out. As we enter there is an absolutely beautiful display of cupcakes, nothing like anything I had seen before. Liz orders a box of 12 and I look at her and she says 'afternoon snack' (yeah right). I order a coffee and wait at a little counter on a barstool.

Liz brings over the box and each different flavour has a different colour dot, and she says you have to try this one first, it's called red velvet. Lucky I was sitting down! OMG what a cupcake! Unlike any other, it's not even fair calling it a cupcake, it's more than that, it's one of the best dessert moments I've ever had, sitting there drinking coffee, me and Liz, perched on high stools eating this moist rich delicate decadent cake and the second you finish it you want another.

We walked all around Beverly Hills looking at shops but what we were really doing was walking off all those cupcakes we had just eaten and that's when the idea of putting the red velvet cupcake mix on a pizza hit me. The one thing that bugged me was I could tell that it wasn't just red food colouring, it was something else in there that gave it the colour and kept it moist and I knew that if

I wanted to try and cook that on a pizza, I had to make sure that it was just as moist when it came out of the oven.

Now, I don't have Sprinkles' exact recipe but this one comes pretty close, you don't just have to use this mix on a pizza, you can make cupcakes with this same recipe. My little secret to this was discovering beetroot juice, which gives the red velvet its distinctive red colour and there is something from the beetroot that's in the juice that makes this really moist. It's the same thing with carrot cake, you wouldn't think putting a vegetable like carrot in a cake would work but it does, and so does the beetroot juice.

PIZZA FUSION

Over four days of driving around LA eating pizza, we kept passing this pizzeria on Sunset Blvd that had all these signs and statements that you normally don't see at a pizzeria. So on our last day, just before we drove to Vegas, we dropped in to see what was going on at Pizza Fusion.

And we were in for a pleasant surprise; we found these guys who are trying to make great pizza, but with a difference. Like their logo says: SAVING THE EARTH ONE PIZZA AT A TIME.

They use fresh certified organic veggies, organic tomato sauce, hormone-free meats, and every pizza is made on white or multigrain pizza bases made with organic flour. Add into the mix organic beer, wine and soft drinks plus they offset all their energy usage, and what you have is somebody who cares about the planet caring about your pizza. We ordered two pizzas:

The Founders – free-range chicken, kalamata olives, roasted red onions, tomato sauce, gorgonzola, mozzarella, provolone and parmesan on an organic white-flour base.

Farmers Market – roasted artichoke hearts, red onions, roasted zucchini, portobello mushrooms, tomato sauce, provolone, mozzarella and parmesan, on a multigrain base.

These pizzas tasted really fresh, not greasy at all, and they were made with love. But what impressed me the most was the wholemeal base; it had a stronger flavour than a normal base but with all those roasted veggies it brought out a really earthy flavour.

2 ROAD TRIP *Los Angeles*

Red velvet

RED VELVET CUPCAKE MIX

60 g unsalted butter, softened
150 g caster sugar
1 extra-large free-range egg
20 ml natural beetroot juice (if you have a juicer, you can make beetroot juice yourself, I use the juice from tinned beetroots)
½ teaspoon vanilla paste
120 ml buttermilk
  (you can make this yourself, p121)
150 g plain flour
½ teaspoon salt
½ teaspoon bicarb soda

CREAM CHEESE ICING

75 g icing sugar, sifted
75 g unsalted butter, softened
75 g cream cheese, softened

1. Mix the butter and sugar on a medium speed until it is all combined. Scrape down the bowl then whisk on highest speed till light and fluffy, about three minutes.
2. Reduce speed to low and add the egg; mix till the egg is completely incorporated.
3. Mix all the liquids together in a separate bowl then at a low speed pour into the butter mixture. Once combined, turn machine off and scrape down, then mix for a further 1 minute.
4. In a separate bowl, combine all the dry ingredients together. On a low speed pour half of the dry ingredients into the wet ingredients and mix for 1 minute. Turn off and scrape down, mix on low again and add the other half of the dry ingredients. Mix for a further minute, stop, scrape down. Mix on medium speed for 1 minute, then on high for 2 minutes.
5. Now the batter is ready for the pizza base or your cupcakes. This mix will make two 10 inch pizzas, or one pizza and 12 cupcakes. For cupcakes, bake at 170°C for 20 minutes.

1. In a mixing bowl place all your ingredients and, using a whisk, mix on a low speed for 1 minute so all the ingredients mix together.
2. Scrape down, turn to high and whisk for 2 minutes.
3. Put mixture into a piping bag with a star nozzle.

2 ROAD TRIP *Los Angeles*

Red velvet

2 basic pizza dough balls – rolled, rested & ready
1 portion of red velvet cupcake mix
1 portion of cream cheese icing

icing sugar for dusting
grated dark chocolate for sprinkling

Pre-heat oven to 220°C

1. Divide the cupcake mix between two pizza bases and, using the back of a spoon, spread evenly, right up to the crust.
2. Bake for 7 minutes. While the pizza is baking, you can make your cream cheese icing.
3. You will know the pizza is ready when a skewer pushed into the centre comes out clean. Take it out of the oven and cut up into 12 pieces.
4. Starting from the outside of the pizza pipe a rose of cream cheese icing on each slice, then a smaller rose closer to the centre. Dust with icing sugar, sprinkle some grated dark chocolate over and serve immediately as the cream cheese will melt if you take too long. This will be a highlight of any pizza party: beautiful, delicate and totally decadent.

Wholemeal pizza bases

I have two wholemeal dough recipes for you to try: one with 100% wholemeal flour, which will be heavy and extra strong in flavour; and one with 70% wholemeal flour and 30% organic white flour for a lighter base but still with that earthy flavour you get from the wholemeal. You can choose whichever you like or, even better, try both and then compare.

Makes eight 200 g pizza dough balls.

100% WHOLEMEAL PIZZA DOUGH

700 ml water
1 tablespoon organic honey
60 g dry instant yeast
20 g salt
1 kg 100% wholemeal flour

70% WHOLEMEAL PIZZA DOUGH

660 ml water
1 tablespoon organic honey
60 g dry instant yeast
20 g salt
700 g wholemeal flour
300 g organic unbleached white flour

1. Pour water into mixing bowl, add honey, place flour on top, then the yeast and salt.

2. Using a dough hook on the lowest speed, mix for 1 minute until combined. Stop and feel the dough: if it sticks to your finger when you poke it, it needs extra flour. You will find that wholemeal flour absorbs more water than white flour.

3. Continue to mix for 7 minutes. Keep an eye on the dough. If it starts to climb up the hook, turn mixer off, push the dough back down to the bottom of the bowl and start again.

4. Remove the bowl from the mixer and cover with cling wrap to stop the dough from forming a skin while the dough rests. You want it to double in size which will take about 1 hour.

5. Knock all of the excess air out of the dough till it is back to normal size. Cut the dough into 8 pieces, weighing 200 g each. Mould into dough balls, cover with a tea towel and leave to rest for 5 minutes, then roll the dough out to the size of your tray. Again, let the dough rest for 1 hour or until it doubles in size, but do not cover the dough as this time you do want it to form a skin – this will help the edges curl up to form your pizza crust.

6. All the time you allow the dough to relax and then knock it back you are creating flavours through the fermentation process and with wholemeal flour you will get an earthy-tasting pizza dough. I find it is best not to hide this flavour with strong toppings, but instead use the flavour of the dough as an added ingredient with toppings that will complement it.

Beverly Hills Grove Farmers Market

This pizza is a combination of influences from the pizzas at Fusion on Sunset and the great fresh food markets that you find popping up all around the States.

You can pretty much buy everything you need for this pizza from your local growers market, and if the ingredients are not in season, you can find great vegetables marinated in oil at good delis.

I will presume that the veggies you are going to use on this pizza are in season, so I will give you a step-by-step run-down on how to grill and marinate each one separately. If you want to try just one of the veggies at a time on a pizza you can, or you can try all of them, it's up to you. These veggies are so good when they are roasted and marinated that you don't only have to use them on a pizza – they make a great starter to any meal or filling in a sandwich.

ROASTED RED CAPSICUM

capsicum (red, green or yellow
 – the process is the same)
garlic, finely chopped
salt
parsley, chopped
extra virgin olive oil

1. On the stove or BBQ place the whole capsicum straight onto the flames (trust me, it is easy and really tasty). Burn one side and turn over until it is fully blackened. Take off flame and wrap loosely in cling wrap.

2. The capsicum will start to sweat and after 10–15 minutes open the cling wrap and rub off the burnt skin with your hands. Leave a little burnt skin on to give the capsicum a great charcoal flavour.

3. Top and halve the capsicum. Scrape out the seeds, cut into strips and place in a bowl with garlic and parsley, a pinch of salt and a drizzle of extra virgin olive oil. Marinate the capsicum while it is still warm (it will absorb more flavours) and leave for a minimum of 10 minutes before using.

ROASTED BUTTERNUT PUMPKIN

½ roasted butternut pumpkin
1 portion of cashew–basil pesto
    150 ml extra virgin olive oil
    1 garlic clove
    30 g parmesan, grated
    30 g unsalted roasted cashews
    125 g fresh basil leaves
    pinch of rock salt

Pre-heat oven to 225°C

1. Peel and deseed your pumpkin, cut into 3 cm strips, place on a baking tray, drizzle with olive oil and sprinkle a pinch of salt.
2. Place in the oven for 10 to 15 minutes. You only want the pumpkin to be semi-cooked as it's going on the pizza where it will cook some more.
3. While your pumpkin is roasting, whip up the cashew–basil pesto by simply placing all the ingredients in a food processor and giving it a whirr.
4. Once cooked, take the pumpkin out of the oven, cut up into cubes and place in a bowl. Add the pesto and mix so all the pumpkin is coated, let it cool before using on the pizza.

MARINATED ZUCCHINI

3 zucchinis
extra virgin olive oil
pinch of salt
pinch of pepper
2 cloves garlic, chopped

Pre-heat oven to 225°C

1. Wash the zucchinis and leave the skin on when roasting. This results in a nice texture and will give your pizza a vibrant green colour.
2. Slice the zucchini length-ways into strips about 1 cm thick and place on a tray. Drizzle with oil, sprinkle a pinch of salt and place in the oven for 5 to 10 minutes.
3. Remove zucchini from oven and cut into chunky slices. Place in a bowl with garlic, a drizzle of extra virgin olive oil and a pinch of salt, stir and let it cool before using.

OVEN ROASTED BEETROOT

beetroots
pinch of salt
pinch of pepper
balsamic vinegar glaze

Pre-heat oven to 225°C

1. Wrap your beetroots in foil and place in the oven for 20 to 30 minutes, depending on the size of the beetroot. The bigger it is, the longer it will take to cook, the smaller the quicker. You can tell when the beetroot is ready by piercing it with a skewer. When the skewer goes in easily, it is done.
2. Take your beetroots out of oven and discard the foil. Peel off the skin, cut into wedges, place in a bowl and sprinkle with a pinch each of salt and pepper and a light drizzle of balsamic vinegar glaze.

2 ROAD TRIP *Los Angeles*

Beverly Hills Grove Farmers Market

This pizza has no sauce on it, it only has the juices of the vegetables and their marinades, and the yogurt on top. You will notice as you are eating the pizza that all the flavours of the vegetables stand out and the yogurt on top gives it a really light fresh zing.

I created the recipe for the readers of LASates.com as a thank you to Ann and Joel for that amazing truffle pizza experience.

1 x 200 g wholemeal dough ball
   – rolled and proofed
90 g mozzarella, grated
½ cup of roasted butternut pumpkin
½ cup roasted red capsicum
½ cup marinated zucchini
½ cup oven roasted beetroot

2 tablespoons Greek yoghurt mixed with fresh chopped chives and squeeze of lemon juice

Pre-heat oven to 250°C

1. Sprinkle the mozzarella evenly around the pizza base.
2. Place the pumpkin, capsicum, zucchini and beetroot on top, making sure that when the pizza is cut, everybody gets a taste of each of the vegetables.
3. Cook for 10 to 15 minutes and when ready, cut up and drizzle Greek yoghurt onto each slice.

CHICAGO
YOU GOTTA FREEZE FOR A GOOD COFFEE

My face is about to fall off it's that cold. I'm walking down Michigan Ave in Chicago, the wind is blowing off Lake Michigan straight at me and I can hardly feel my nose and toes. It is so so cold, it's snowing and it's -3°C. Hard to believe that only seven days ago I was at work in Perth melting in the kitchen on a 37°C night with no relief in sight, and here I am now freezing my balls off. The locals tell me that they are going into spring, but I think they are all on drugs: this is arctic weather and only good for penguins. What I need to find now is a good cup of boiling hot coffee.

Intelligentsia is the place to go for great coffee in Chicago. They have an espresso machine but most of the coffee sold is Chemex brewed coffee or from a syphon brewer – very geeky but great coffee, no sugar necessary: it is that clean and crisp.

That became my ritual every day in Chicago: a seven-minute walk in the snow for one of the best coffees ever. Tough call, stay at the hotel nice and warm near a fire and drink bad coffee or freeze for the great stuff.

The main reason I was in Chicago was to do a cooking demonstration at the International Home & Housewares Show, which is a massive show running over three days for the industry only. I was appearing at the cooking theatre with some of the greats, Mario Batali, Cat Cora, Paula Deen, Michael Symon, Rick Bayless, Guy Fieri, Ming Tsai, Todd English, Masaharu Morimoto and Curtis Stone. They all may be well-known celebrity chefs but the one thing that I saw over the three days was all of them loving what they do: cooking.

THE CHICAGO DEEP DISH PIZZA

The one thing that I wanted to learn while I was in Chicago was a style of pizza that you cannot find anywhere else. Love it or hate it, it's been around since 1943 and it ain't going away, it's the Chicago deep dish pizza.

The place I started my journey to find out how to make this deep-dish pizza was at Uno's, the first pizzeria in Chicago to make it. As I was walking down to Uno's I passed a big pizza chain that will remain nameless and it was nearly empty and only a few doors up was Uno's with a line coming out of the door into the cold Chicago night. As I got to the front of the line they told me it will be a one-hour wait and as a Chicago-style pizza takes 45 minutes to bake they take your pizza order first so it can start baking and by the time you get to your table, your pizza will be ready. (That's your first tip: a Chicago deep-dish pizza requires a long and slow bake)

We get called to our table and as we order some drinks the waitress tells us that our pizza will be ready in about 10 minutes.

The pizza arrives. I ordered a medium deep-dish spinach pizza, it's like nothing I've seen before. I'm really excited to pull this pizza apart so I can try to make it at home, and the first thing I notice is that the sauce is on top. (This is your second tip: put the sauce on top to stop the base from getting soggy).

As I start eating I realize that having the sauce on top works as the base is still well-baked and crispy. It's not like a normal pizza dough, more like a short crust dough and it has a very different bite to it and a different texture as you eat it – it crumbles in your mouth with a very rich, buttery flavour. The finger marks I see in the crust tell me that the dough was pushed into the tray rather than rolled out. (Third tip: don't use a rolling pin but instead push the dough out with the palm of your hand and your fingers).

This pizza has a very homemade feel about it, even though they make hundreds of them every day.

2 ROAD TRIP *Chicago*

Chicago deep dish pizza dough

This recipe makes 1.3 kg dough which is enough for a big and a small deep dish Chicago pizza. The tin I used was round, 30 cm diameter and 2.5 cm deep.

Made as one whole pizza this is so heavy that it could feed an army with a light salad. You have to eat Chicago deep dish pizza with a knife and fork sitting down, it is very thick, very cheesy and really good. The first time I made this for my brother Tass he said it reminded him of something a Nonna would make. He took the leftovers home for lunch at work the next day.

440 ml water
40 g butter
200 ml olive oil
600 g plain flour (8% protein)
70 g fine semolina
20 g dry yeast
1 teaspoon salt
1 teaspoon sugar
1 tablespoon olive oil for rubbing the dough just before proofing

1. Using a mixer with a dough hook, place water, butter and olive oil into the mixing bowl. Then place half flour, half the semolina, all the yeast, salt, and sugar and mix for 3 to 4 minutes until all the ingredients make a nice smooth batter. Remove and cover the bowl with a tea towel or cling wrap and leave to rest for 20 minutes.

2. Return bowl to mixer, add remaining flour and semolina, and mix on low speed for 7 minutes.

3. Take the slightly yellow dough and divide into $\frac{2}{3}$ for a big pan and $\frac{1}{3}$ for a small pan, if you have an extra-large pan use it all. It will be a soft and tacky dough, looking more like a batter. Mould the dough into a smooth ball and rub evenly with the extra olive oil. Place it in a large bowl and cover with a tea towel and let it rest for 1 hour.

4. Put about a teaspoon of olive oil in your deep dish pan and use a brush to coat the surface entirely. Grab your dough ball and place it in the middle of the pan, and using your fingers and palm, push and spread the dough evenly around the pan, getting it to about 2 cm from the top as you push it up the edge of the tray. Once you have done that, cover the pan with a teatowel and let it rest for 30 minutes. Now it is ready to use.

I know you are thinking what a long process and it is, but Chicago deep dish pizza is like no other and you need to go through these stages to get that flaky rich crust. It really is a combination of a quiche base and a pizza base, so if you want to make it you need to follow these guidelines; if not, then I think a trip to Chicago is your only other option.

Chicago deep dish spinach

CHICAGO DEEP DISH TOMATO SAUCE

20 ml olive oil
1 tin whole peeled tomatoes 400 g
$\frac{1}{2}$ teaspoon dried oregano
$\frac{1}{4}$ teaspoon salt
1 clove garlic, finely chopped
1 teaspoon dried basil leaves

PIZZA

14 inch deep pan with Chicago deep dish dough ready to go
1 portion Chicago deep dish tomato sauce
500 g mozzarella, sliced (not grated, must be big thin slices)
150 g baby spinach, washed and patted dry
2 cloves garlic, finely chopped
pinch pepper
pinch salt
60 g parmesan cheese, grated

Pre-heat oven to 230°C

1. Place olive oil and the tomatoes into a saucepan over medium heat, stir and crush the tomatoes with the back of a fork as you are cooking them.

2. When the tomatoes are crushed, add the oregano, salt, garlic and basil, stir it all together and let it simmer for about 30 minutes on a low heat. The sauce should reduce and become nice and thick.

3. Once it has cooled down it is ready to use.

1. The first thing you do is start by laying half of the sliced mozzarella on the bottom of your deep dish dough, by using sliced cheese and not grated it acts as a barrier so no liquid flows down to the bottom like it would if the cheese was grated.

2. In a separate bowl place the spinach, garlic, salt and pepper and mix together then place into the pan on top of the cheese. Place the rest of the cheese evenly over the spinach then spoon the tomato sauce onto the slices of mozzarella and spread evenly. The final stage is to sprinkle the grated parmesan over the pizza sauce, now it is ready to go in the oven.

3. Bake in the centre of the oven (fan off), without opening the door for about 30 minutes, then have a look: it may need another 5 minutes. You are after a really golden crust and a bubbling sauce with golden brown melted cheese.

4. Once you have taken the pizza out of the oven let it sit in the pan for 5 minutes before you serve it. Like lasagna, the deep pan pizza needs this time to sit so it stops cooking and it all comes together. After 5 minutes make sure that all the crust has come away from the edges of the pan, if not, use a knife to push the crust away from the edge. Use a flat spatula to cut your pizza up into slices in the pan – it is easier to use a spatula but you can use a knife. Place the whole deep dish in the middle of the table and let everyone serve themselves straight out of the Chicago deep dish pan.

COMING HOME

As crazy as it seems, travelling 33 hours to get home goes really fast when you know how to do it. It also helps knowing that Liz and Chaz will be at the airport to pick me up, and even though I haven't slept much, and I need a shower, all I want to do is talk to them and catch up with what's been going on. Even the most boring things mean a lot when you are away for 3 to 4 weeks working. I always try to take Liz or Chaz with me whenever they can, it makes it so much better, but it's not always possible; Chaz needs to go to school and Liz is busy running the house and the pizzerias.

It's a really odd feeling after a day or two of being home, it's like I never left, but it also feels like I'm still there. It takes a while to fit in again back home, sometimes I think if I got a phone call the day after I've arrived from America asking me to go back because some work has popped up, I could get on a plane and go straight back without a worry. But I think that's probably because I know home is here for me and always will be.

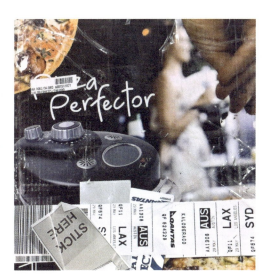

3 HOME SWEET HOME

I love being home with Liz and Chaz. Cooking a nice lazy late breakfast, Chaz having some friends over in the afternoon for a swim and some food, then some friends stopping round later in the evening. It is great to take the time to cook at home. I know, yeah, I cook for work so why would I cook at home? But I love it and what better way to spend time with your family and friends than feeding them all a feast you have cooked yourself?

If there is one food that is perfect for a party, that is loved by so many people, that can cater for everybody from vegetarians to meat lovers, seafoodtarians, celiac and lactose intolerant friends, then it's pizza. Imagine having a party for fifty people and trying to feed them all – it's a lot of work, but if I'm going to have a party and invite all of the above then I'm not going to be stuck in the kitchen cooking special meals. No, I'm going to be in the middle of it all cooking, eating and enjoying myself.

You'll be amazed how versatile pizza is. And to have a party, you simply:

- Send the invites out
- Buy your ingredients
- Do all the prep in the morning
- Get your oven hot
- Start cooking
- Let the guests make their own and ... ENJOY!

BREAKFAST

Cooking a lazy breakfast is a nice
start to a day off work.
At my house breakfast pizza often
becomes brunch instead,
but trust me, that's okay too!
The point is to relax with the
people you love and to enjoy life,
and what better way to do that
than to cook and eat together?

So, what's it going to be?
Eggs Florentine, perhaps?
Or the quirky Jebediah –
a doughnut-style pizza complete
with an affogato?

Eggs Florentine

STEAMED AND SPICED BABY SPINACH

1 really big handful of baby spinach
1 garlic clove, finely minced
½ teaspoon fresh ginger, grated
pinch of salt
pinch of pepper

PIZZA

1 basic pizza dough ball – rolled, rested & ready
1 cup low fat mozzarella, grated
1 portion steamed & spiced spinach
3 free range eggs

Sour cream hollandaise
1 tablespoon fresh chives, finely chopped
pinch of pepper

SOUR CREAM HOLLANDAISE

3 tablespoons of light sour cream
juice of 1 lemon
1 tablespoon fresh parsley, chopped
pinch of pepper

Pre-heat oven to 220°C

1. Place the baby spinach in a pot of boiling water for one minute.
2. Take out and strain.
3. In a bowl mix the spinach with the garlic, ginger, salt and pepper and set aside.

1. Roll out your pizza dough ball to fit the tray, sprinkle mozzarella evenly around pizza base, place spinach mix on top and then crack eggs onto the pizza. Place in the oven to cook for 7 to 10 minutes.

   HOT TIP to keep the eggs from running all over the pizza, use the back of a tablespoon and make a dent in the spinach then crack the egg into the indentations so the yolk stays there.

2. While your pizza is cooking, make the sour cream hollandaise.
3. When cooked, remove pizza from oven, cut into 12 pieces and place on a serving tray. Then dollop a teaspoon of sour cream hollandaise onto each slice and top with a sprinkle of chopped chives.

1. Place all the ingredients into a bowl and whisk together until smooth and evenly mixed.

   This is a breakfast pizza that won't make you feel guilty if you have another piece. By replacing the hollandaise sauce with a sour cream sauce this becomes a healthy breakfast of champions. It has great flavours and it is good for you.

3 HOME SWEET HOME *Breakfast*

Green eggs & ham

This is one of those funny recipes chefs like to play with: what were those eggs that Dr Seuss's Sam would not eat but then loved? This is my version, and it is another classic flavour combination turned into a pizza.

1 pizza dough ball – rolled, rested & ready
1 teaspoon garlic, chopped
90 g mozzarella, grated
100 g shaved ham
2 cups fresh baby spinach leaves, washed and patted dry
3 tablespoons cream sauce (p166)
1 egg
pinch of salt
pinch of pepper

50 ml whole egg mayonnaise (p136)

Pre-heat oven to 220°C

1. Crack your egg in a bowl with a pinch of salt and pepper. Add the cream sauce and whisk together.
2. Sprinkle garlic over your pizza base, then place your shaved ham, top with mozzarella and spinach leaves. Sprinkle a pinch of salt and pepper over the whole pizza, and drizzle the whisked egg mix in a swirl over the pizza (if you want a whole egg on your pizza, use the back of a tablespoon to make a dent in the spinach, this will help contain your egg).
3. Cook for 7 to 10 minutes.
4. Drizzle the whole-egg mayonnaise around the pizza and serve.

3 HOME SWEET HOME *Breakfast*

Jebediah

The flavours of this pizza are inspired by the great wordsmith, Homer Simpson, and his love for coffee and doughnuts.

1 basic pizza dough ball – rolled, rested & ready (and a 50 mm metal cookie cutter to make the doughnut hole)
65 g unsalted butter, softened
$\frac{1}{2}$ cup caster sugar
$\frac{1}{2}$ teaspoon vanilla paste
$\frac{1}{2}$ teaspoon ground cinnamon
1 eggs
1 cup self raising flour
1 tablespoon cinnamon sugar

1 affogato (espresso coffee poured over vanilla bean ice-cream in a small cup)

Pre-heat oven to 220°C

1 Cream together butter and sugar on medium speed for one minute, scrape down.

2 Add vanilla, ground cinnamon and egg and mix on low speed for one minute, scrape down.

3 Add flour and mix on low speed for one minute, scrape down, then mix on medium speed for another minute.

4 Creating a doughnut hole in your pizza is easy. Get your pizza base and push a 50 mm metal cookie cutter into the middle of it and leave it there until the pizza is cooked.

5 Spread the batter right up to the cookie cutter (remember you will be pulling this out later to give you the doughnut hole). Sprinkle over one tablespoon of cinnamon sugar.

6 Cook for 7 minutes.

7 When cooked, use tongs to rip out the cookie cutter, place your affogato in the middle of the hole, and serve with spoons so you can have coffee and doughnuts at the same time.

Mmm doughnuts....

STARTERS

Every culture has its own type of simple bread and many are made in ways similar to pizza. So using your pizza making skills and your pizza oven, you can make delicious breads for dips and starters.

For example, manakish is a flat bread found throughout the Middle East from Lebanon to Syria, Jordan and Palestine; in Arabic they pronounce it Manaeesh, and it is served at all meals but with different toppings. So for breakfast it is topped with zatar (see p173), at lunch it is topped with akkawi cheese (an Arabic cheese with a creamy flavour and texture similar to that of mozzarella), and at dinner it will be topped with minced lamb and served with a side of yoghurt and some fresh cucumber and tomatoes.

Of course, the traditional Australian starter to go with pizza is garlic bread, and nothing beats fresh garlic bread made from scratch.

3 HOME SWEET HOME *Starters*

Butter

Making your own garlic bread is very easy and lots of people do it, but making your own garlic butter from scratch is more unusual. I'm going to give you a recipe for a different style of garlic bread and a recipe for garlic butter that you can make from scratch or, if you want, you can buy butter and mix in the flavours – either way, this is a great twist on normal, boring garlic bread.

Have you ever whipped cream and forgot about it and, when you came back to it, it had started to separate? When there is milky liquid floating around and the cream is at the point of no return and it's all lumpy and turning yellow? Well, don't stop! You are on the way to making butter, and that milky liquid is buttermilk, get it? Keep mixing until it turns yellow and smooth.

Cream is all you need to make butter at home, so it's not the ingredients that will put you off making butter yourself, it's the process. But if you have got time it's well worth it, and you will definitely taste the difference.

600 ml fresh cream (yields ~300 g butter)

1. Place the fresh cream in a mixing bowl and begin to whisk on medium-high, making sure you are not splattering cream all over the kitchen.

2. Mix for 3 minutes then speed the mixer up to high; at this stage the cream looks like it is about to curdle (looking like ricotta)

3. At the five minute mark a liquid will start to come out of the cream. Turn off the mixer at six minutes.

4. Sieve the butter and excess liquid into a bowl so you can catch the liquid, this is buttermilk. You only get it from the first step of turning cream into butter and you can keep this to add to pancakes or any recipe asking for buttermilk (like the red velvet cupcakes, p92).

5. Place the butter back into the mixing bowl, add 500 ml of cold water and mix on a low speed until the water becomes cloudy, about one minute. Do this three times, straining the cloudy water out of the mixing bowl and adding 500 ml of cold water each time.

6. You should have a nice soft yellowy butter on the third and final mix. Let it strain for five minutes before putting the butter back into your rinsed and wiped mixing bowl.

7. Now you are ready to add all the ingredients to turn this butter into whipped garlic butter.

3 HOME SWEET HOME *Starters*

Garlic bread

GARLIC BUTTER

Use the butter you have just made, or use 250 g of store-bought butter
1 clove fresh garlic, finely chopped
1 tablespoon fresh parsley, chopped
1 teaspoon salt
big pinch cracked black pepper

GARLIC BREAD

550 ml cold water
50 ml extra virgin olive oil
1 kg strong bakers flour
20 g dry instant yeast
10 g salt
10 g sugar
1 tablespoon rock salt
1 teaspoon black pepper
fresh garlic, finely chopped
fresh parsley, finely chopped

sesame seeds
black sesame seeds

Pre-heat oven to 220°C

1. Place everything in the mixing bowl with the butter and whisk until all the ingredients have been evenly distributed and the butter is light and fluffy.

2. Place mixture in a piping bag with a star nozzle at the end and pipe out into little ramekins.

3. When finished, place the ramekins in the fridge so the butter goes hard. Now you are ready to start your garlic bread.

1. Place water and oil into the mixing bowl, followed by flour, yeast, salt and sugar, and mix for seven minutes.

2. Turn off machine and add garlic, parsley, salt and pepper and mix for another three minutes.

3. Take the dough out of the bowl and cut up into eight pieces weighing 200 g each. Shape into balls and leave to rest for five minutes and then roll out to the size of an extra small pizza (about 8 inch).

4. Using a knife, score the rolled out dough like a pizza into 8 pieces but do not cut all the way through. Brush the top of the dough with the olive oil and sprinkle sesame seeds on top. Cover with a tea towel and let the dough triple in size.

5. Cook (fan off) for 7 minutes and then check top and bottom to see if the bread is cooked, it should be a deep, golden colour and sound hollow when tapped.

6. When ready, place on a tray to serve and put a garlic butter ramekin in the middle so each person can spread what ever amount of butter they want on the garlic bread.

CARNIVORE

Chicken and bacon are both well-loved pizza toppings in Australia, and I have some great recipes here for you using both, including the Black Box on page 57, and Tribeca on page 71. But I also love the non-traditional pizza because it opens up new possibilities and that inspires me like, for example, the wood-fired pork loin on page 61 or the pork belly on sourdough on page 83 and the Classica with fennel sausage on page 7. I hope you enjoy the flavour combinations I have come up with for kangaroo and speck and pork. Try them all and make your tastebuds happy!

3 HOME SWEET HOME *Carnivore*

BBQ plate

BBQ SAUCE

- 1 tablespoon olive oil
- 1 bacon rasher
- 1 sprig of fresh rosemary, same length as the bacon rasher
- ½ onion, finely chopped
- 1 clove of garlic, finely chopped
- 1 bottle (300 ml) tomato sauce
- 60 g brown sugar
- 3 tablespoons red wine vinegar
- 2 teaspoons smoked paprika
- pinch of salt
- pinch of pepper

CARAMELISED ONIONS

- 1 tablespoon olive oil
- 1 tablespoon butter
- 1 tablespoon brown sugar
- 500 g red onions – peeled, halfed & thinly sliced

PIZZA

- 1 pizza dough ball – rolled, rested & ready
- 90 g mozzarella, grated
- 30 g smoked ham, shaved
- 80 g pepper steak, cooked and sliced
- 80 g roasted chicken, shredded
- 40 g caramelised onions
- 60 ml (3 tablespoons) BBQ sauce

- 1 teaspoon fresh parsley, chopped

Pre-heat oven to 220°C

You can buy good BBQ sauce – it's out there – but here is a recipe with a distinctive smoky flavour.

1. Pour oil into a non-stick pan on medium heat, wrap bacon around rosemary and put into pan. You want the bacon to get some colour.
2. Add onion and cook for two minutes, you don't want to burn the onions so be careful. Add garlic and cook for another minute. Turn up the heat, add the remaining ingredients and stir till the sugar has dissolved. When the sauce starts to boil lower the heat and simmer for 10 minutes.
3. Turn off and leave the sauce in the pan to cool down then strain off the big bits before using. The sauce will keep in the fridge up to seven days.

1. In a pan over a medium heat, heat the oil and melt your butter. Add onions and cook until they are translucent and soft, about 10 minutes – you want to cook them slowly so as not to burn them.
2. Add in the brown sugar and turn off the heat. Stir together and let the residual heat from the onions melt the sugar.
3. Let them cool and they are ready for your pizza. Caramelised onions will keep up to seven days in the fridge.

This pizza takes three distinctive flavours and combines them with a smokey BBQ sauce for the ultimate BBQ pizza.

1. Spread the mozzarella evenly over the pizza base. Add shaved ham, pepper steak and roast chicken. Top with caramelised onions and then swirl BBQ sauce on top.
2. Cook 7 to 10 minutes. When ready cut, sprinkle with parsley and serve.

3 HOME SWEET HOME *Carnivore*

Roast chicken burrito

This pizza takes the essence and the flavours of a Mexican burrito and instead of rolling it all up, puts it on a pizza base.

SPICY TOMATO SALSA

200 g fresh tomatoes, washed, cored and cubed to remove excess water
200 g tinned whole peeled tomatoes
1 garlic clove
1 teaspoon fresh coriander leaves
1 fresh hot thin red chilli, topped & de-seeded
1 teaspoon extra virgin olive oil
1 green capsicum, topped & de-seeded
big pinch of salt
pinch of black pepper

1. Place all ingredients in a blender (if you don't have one just chop everything into small cubes).
2. Blitz till all ingredients are chopped and you have a nice thick sauce.
3. Place in a bowl and put in the fridge for minimum of one hour. You can make this the day before to give all the flavours time develop.

ACHIOTE-MARINATED CHICKEN

chicken pieces
Achiote (available from specialty shops and online. You can substitute by making a paste of plain paprika, a pinch of salt and a bit of oil).

1. Marinate your chicken pieces in achiote. Achiote is a paste made from annatto seeds, and once you add water it becomes a vibrant red color. When it covers the chicken pieces you will get extra flavoursome, colourful chicken. Leave to marinate for 5 minutes.
2. Roast your chicken pieces in the oven or cook them on the BBQ. Once cooled down, dice the chicken meat.

Roast chicken burrito

PICO DE GALLO

1 tomato, diced
1 small green chilli, diced
1 tablespoon coriander, finely chopped
½ red onion, diced
pinch of salt

GUACAMOLE

1 large avocado, mashed
1 tablespoon coriander, finely chopped
½ red onion, finely diced
1 lime, juiced
pinch of salt
pinch of pepper

PIZZA

1 basic pizza dough ball – rolled, rested & ready
2 tablespoons spicy tomato salsa
1 cup low fat mozzarella, grated
1 portion achiote-marinated chicken
2 tablespoons black beans (tinned, so drain and wash; kidney beans also work)
2 tablespoons red onion, thinly sliced

pico de gallo ('rooster's beak', a fresh salsa)
guacamole

Pre-heat oven to 220°C

1. Place all ingredients in a bowl, mix with a spoon and set aside.

1. Place all ingredients in a bowl, mix with a spoon and set aside.

1. Spread the spicy tomato salsa evenly over the base, then cover with mozzarella. Place chicken pieces on top of mozzarella and sprinkle with black beans. Top with thinly sliced red onion.
2. Cook for 7 to 10 minutes.
3. Once cooked, cut the pizza into 12 pieces and place on serving dish with a spoonful of the fresh Pico de Gallo on each piece – this will add a light and fresh flavour to the pizza.
4. Serve with guacamole on the side for those who want to dollop some onto their piece of pizza.

3 HOME SWEET HOME *Carnivore*

Kangaroo with crème fraiche & pomegranate

This pizza should be made when pomegranates are in season; usually they are available from autumn to the end of winter. If they're out of season and you want to make this pizza without fresh pomegranate you can use pomegranate molasses, which is great.

If your kangaroo fillets are of uneven thickness, use a mallet and tap them till they are all evenly thin before slicing into strips. Use kangaroo like you would any other lean meat, and don't be afraid of it. If you are using frozen kangaroo, make sure it is fully defrosted otherwise it will release excess water when it is cooking on your pizza.

SPICED KANGAROO FILLETS

2 kangaroo fillets
extra virgin olive oil
1 teaspoon coriander seeds
1 teaspoon cumin seeds
1 teaspoon sea salt

PIZZA

1 basic pizza dough ball – rolled, rested & ready
½ garlic clove, finely chopped
90 g mozzarella, grated
100 g spiced kangaroo fillets, sliced
½ cup caramelised onions (p127)

crème fraiche
fresh basil leaves
pomegranate kernels

Pre-heat oven to 220–250 °C

1 Place coriander, cumin and sea salt in a mortar and crush together.

2 Cut the fillets into strips and toss them in a drizzle of extr no thinner than 5 mm a virgin olive oil.

3 Coat them in the spice mixture and they are ready to go on the pizza.

1 Sprinkle the chopped garlic over the pizza base then add the mozzarella. Arrange the sliced and spiced kangaroo fillet and then top with caramelised onions.

2 Cook for 10 minutes.

3 When ready, cut the pizza into eight pieces, top with a dollop of crème fraiche on each slice and a few leaves of basil. Sprinkle pomegranate kernels around the pizza and serve.

3 HOME SWEET HOME *Carnivore*

Birds of Tokyo

This Perth band is a favourite of mine so I was happy when I could combine the tastes of Japan to create a pizza in their honour.

1 pizza dough ball – rolled, rested & ready
1 teaspoon garlic, finely chopped
90 g mozzarella, grated
230 g roasted chicken, cut into pieces
50 ml teriyaki sauce
2 tablespoons sesame seeds

100 g pickled cucumber, thinly sliced
50 ml Japanese mayonnaise
1 teaspoon fresh parsley, chopped

Pre-heat oven to 220°C

1. Place the chicken and teriyaki sauce in a bowl and mix. Let it sit for five minutes before using.

2. Sprinkle garlic and then mozzarella evenly around pizza base, place marinated chicken on top and then sprinkle sesame seeds all over the chicken. When the pizza cooks, the seeds will start to toast and they will add a nice nutty flavour.

3. Cook for 7 to 10 minutes

4. Cut into eight pieces, and top with the pickled cucumbers. Make sure you place an even amount on each piece. Swirl the Japanese mayonnaise over the pizza and sprinkle with parsley to serve.

BLAT – bacon-lettuce-avocado-tomato

This pizza is different, because more ingredients go on the pizza once it comes out of the oven than go on it before it is cooked – this pizza is like eating a salad and a pizza at the same time.

WHOLE-EGG MAYONNAISE

1 egg-yolk
1 cup of oil
½ teaspoon salt
2 teaspoons lemon juice

PIZZA

1 basic pizza dough ball – rolled, rested & ready
1 teaspoon garlic, finely chopped
90 g mozzarella, grated
100 g fresh tomato, sliced no thicker than 1cm
pinch of salt

140 g bacon, cooked till crispy
8 baby cos lettuce leaves
½ avocado, sliced into 8 even pieces
50 ml whole-egg mayonnaise

Pre-heat oven to 220°C

1. Begin by whisking the egg yolk. Drizzle in the oil very slowly allowing the egg to incorporate the oil. Continue until all the oil is gone, you will know when it is ready as the mixture should be thick enough to stick to your whisk. Add the salt and lemon juice and mix gently into the mayonnaise.

   This is a basic recipe – you can add garlic, chives, saffron etc. to come up with your own special mayonnaise – it takes only a few minutes to make, but it may take several attempts to make it properly.

1. Sprinkle the garlic and then the mozzarella evenly over the pizza base, then top with the fresh tomato and a pinch of salt.
2. Cook for 5 to 7 minutes
3. Cut into 8 pieces. Place one cos lettuce leaf with a slice of avocado in it, on each pizza slice, sprinkle crispy bacon evenly over the pizza and swirl the whole-egg mayonnaise over to serve. Then enjoy a really fresh and crispy salad pizza.

Speck & peas

The smoky saltiness of speck combined with the juicy peas and the cream sauce makes this a very easy crowd-pleaser.

1 basic pizza dough ball – rolled, rested & ready
1 tablespoon garlic, finely chopped
80 g mozzarella, grated
110 g speck, cut into 3 cm strips
$\frac{1}{4}$ cup (40 g) peas
3 tablespoons cream sauce (p166)

pinch of salt
pinch of pepper
fresh parsley, chopped

Pre-heat oven to 220°C

1. Sprinkle garlic evenly over the base then top with mozzarella. Place speck on pizza, sprinkle the peas around, and then drizzle with cream sauce.
2. Cook for 7 to 10 minutes
3. When ready, cut into eight pieces and crack some salt and pepper over, then sprinkle with parsley and serve.

3 HOME SWEET HOME *Carnivore*

Chicken & leek

The flavour combination of roast chicken, bacon and leek drizzled with cream sauce is perfect with a crisp white wine.

1 basic pizza dough ball – rolled, rested & ready
1 teaspoon garlic, finely chopped
90 g mozzarella, grated
130 g roasted chicken, diced
75 g bacon pieces
30 g leek, cleaned & cut into 1 cm slices
3 tablespoons cream sauce (p166)
pinch of salt
pinch of pepper

1 teaspoon fresh thyme leaves

Pre-heat oven to 220°C

1. Sprinkle garlic over pizza base then top with mozzarella. Place chicken and bacon evenly around, top with leek, drizzle cream sauce over and add a pinch of salt and pepper.
2. Cook for 7 to 10 minutes
3. Cut and sprinkle thyme leaves over and serve.

Cinnamon Girl

This pizza is inspired by the flavours of North Africa: cinnamon, sweet potato and sultanas — oh yeah, and I got the name from a song by Neil Young … *I could be happy the rest of my life with a cinnamon girl …*

1 basic pizza dough ball – rolled, rested & ready
30 g sultanas
90 g mozzarella, grated
150 g roasted chicken, diced
1 teaspoon cinnamon
80 g sweet potato – roasted, peeled and cut into thin strips
3 tablespoons cream sauce (p166)
pinch of salt

drizzle of balsamic glaze
1 teaspoon fresh parsley or chives, chopped

Pre-heat oven to 220°C

1. Mix the chicken and cinnamon in a bowl.
2. Place sultanas on the pizza base (you need to put them under the mozzarella as they will burn if they are on top). Sprinkle mozzarella evenly and top with cinnamon chicken. Place sweet potato strips evenly around, drizzle cream sauce and add a pinch of salt.
3. Cook for 7 to 10 minutes
4. When ready, cut and swirl balsamic glaze over pizza then sprinkle with parsley or chives and it is ready to eat.

3 HOME SWEET HOME *Carnivore*

Pork & sage

I use a fresh pork and sage sausage for this recipe. If you can't find any, don't sweat it, just use your favourite pork sausage.

1 basic pizza dough ball – rolled, rested & ready
2 pork & sage sausages
90 g mozzarella, grated
½ green apple – peeled, cored and sliced thin
1 teaspoon brown sugar
40 g sweet potato – peeled, roasted and sliced thin

1 teaspoon olive oil
8 fresh sage leaves

Pre-heat oven to 220°C

1. Drizzle the oil into a pan on a medium heat and add your fresh sage leaves – they will start to fry quickly (in seconds). When they start to curl and go crispy, take them out, place on paper towel to absorb the oil and put aside.

2. Now put your sausages into the same pan and cook for a few minutes. You are trying to get some nice colour on the outside of your sausages but you only want to cook them ¾ of the way, as they will finish cooking in the oven on your pizza. When ready, take them out and leave to cool down, then cut them into bite-sized pieces.

3. Spread mozzarella evenly on pizza base, place your bite-sized pieces of pork sausage around, fill in the spaces with the sliced apple – your apple pieces should look like a half-moon – sprinkle the brown sugar over the apple, top with sweet potato.

4. Cook for 7 to 10 minutes.

5. When ready cut into eight pieces, place a crispy fried sage leaf on each pizza slice and serve.

ated & ready

Pork star

This pizza is proof that you don't need an expensive cut of meat for a really great pizza.

PORK MINCE

180 g pork mince
2 tablespoons of olive oil
1 teaspoon of black pepper
1 teaspoon rock salt
1 teaspoon fennel seeds

PIZZA

1 basic pizza dough ball – rolled, rested & ready
1 teaspoon garlic, finely chopped
90 g mozzarella, grated
110 g pork mince, cooked
80 g sweet potato – peeled, roasted and cut into strips
40 g caramelised onions (p122)
pinch of salt

$\frac{1}{2}$ teaspoon fennel seeds, crushed
1 teaspoon fresh parsley, chopped

Pre-heat oven to 220°C

1. Crush the spices using a mortar and pestle into a powder, add to the pork and mix through.
2. Drizzle the olive oil into a pan over medium heat and add pork mince.
3. The pork won't take long to cook – about 3 to 5 minutes. Let it cool before using on pizza.

1. Sprinkle the garlic over the pizza base and top with mozzarella. Spread the pork mince evenly around. Top with sweet potato and then onions.
2. Cook for 7 to 10 minutes
3. When ready, cut into eight pieces, sprinkle the crushed fennel seeds and the parsley over the pizza and it is ready to eat.

3 HOME SWEET HOME *Carnivore*

Portuguese chicken

The peri peri spice-mix has its origins in Portugal and is made up of crushed chillies, citrus peel, onion, garlic, pepper, salt, lemon juice, bay leaves, paprika, pimiento, basil, oregano, and tarragon).

1 basic pizza dough ball – rolled, rested & ready
90 g mozzarella, grated
150 g roasted chicken, diced
1 teaspoon paprika
3 tablespoons peri peri sauce, or use the spicy tomato sauce recipe on p170 and just add 1 teaspoon of Spanish smoky paprika
60 g white onion, thinly sliced
60 g roasted red capsicum, sliced
pinch of salt

1 teaspoon fresh parsley, chopped

Pre-heat oven to 220°C

1. Mix chicken, paprika and peri peri sauce together in bowl and let it sit for five minutes.

2. Spread the mozzarella over the pizza base, then place the marinated chicken. Top with onions and red capsicum and a pinch of salt.

3. Cook for 7-10 minutes.

4. When ready, cut into eight pieces, sprinkle parsley over and serve.

SEAFOOD

We have great seafood in Australia and what better place to enjoy it than on top of a pizza? There are recipes here for pizzas with smoked salmon, tuna, sardines, and prawns, lots of prawns, I love my prawns – and while you plan your seafood pizza menu, don't forget the spectacular New York-style clams on page 67, and the Sicilian swordfish on page 12.

3 HOME SWEET HOME *Seafood*

Flaming lips

I'm not sure if it was in Singapore or Hong Kong when I first ate wonderful spicy tuna sushi. However, it wasn't till I was in Cape Town in South Africa, at the waterfront having the freshest and best spicy sushi that I've ever had that it clicked with me to use these flavours on a pizza. I don't know what it was that caused this madness – maybe because I was in a different city or that it was so good it triggered something. Anyway, my taste buds loved it and finally a light went on in my head and I came up with my combination of ingredients and flavours with the same tastes they use in the sushi in Cape Town.

It is spicy but it's not blow-your-head-off hot, more like flavourfully spicy.

The ingredient that really makes this pizza is the Sriracha chilli sauce. You can find it everywhere – it's the bottle with the rooster on it. The sauce is made from sun-ripened chillies that are ground with vinegar, salt, garlic and sugar; it is a sweet hot sauce.

Shichimi Togarashi is a traditional Japanese seven-pepper spice mix.

1 basic pizza dough ball – rolled, rested & ready
120 g tuna steak, grilled lightly and cubed
    (or just use tinned tuna slices)
1 tablespoon garlic, finely chopped
1 teaspoon Shichimi Togarashi
    (or ordinary chilli flakes)
90 g mozzarella, grated
80 g red onion, finely sliced

Japanese mayonnaise
Sriracha (Rooster Sauce) chilli sauce
1 tablespoon dried seaweed, finely chopped

Pre-heat oven to 220°C

1. If you are using a fresh tuna steak, grill it on each side for a minute to get grill marks. You are not trying to cook the tuna as it is going to get cooked on the pizza. If you don't have tuna steaks, tinned tuna slices are fine, so don't think it won't work: it will taste the same, it is just a visual thing and a different texture.

2. Place the tuna into a bowl. Add the chopped garlic and Shichimi Togarashi and mix together. Leave to marinate for 10 minutes before using.

3. To assemble, spread garlic over pizza base then top with mozzarella. Place your tuna pieces over the mozzarella and sprinkle with Shicimi Togarashi and red onions.

4. Cook for 7 to 10 minutes.

5. When ready, cut into eight pieces, then from the centre of each slice place a strip of mayo and chilli sauce next to each other running from the point to the crust of the pizza (like the GT stripes on the bonnet of a car), sprinkle finely chopped seaweed, dig in...and try not to get any on your lips!

3 HOME SWEET HOME *Seafood*

Puttanesca

The traditional flavours of the pasta sauce puttanesca – salty, spicy and fragrant – are even more amazing as a pizza.

1 basic pizza dough ball – rolled, rested & ready
1 teaspoon garlic, finely chopped
90 g mozzarella, grated
80 g marinated sardines (I use Fremantle sardines)
1 teaspoon baby capers
30 g olives, pitted and halved
8 cherry tomatoes, halved
2 tablespoons basic pizza sauce (p33)
pinch of salt
½ teaspoon dried chilli flakes
1 teaspoon dried oregano

1 lemon, cut into wedges

Pre-heat oven to 220°C

1. Spread the garlic over the pizza base and then top with mozzarella. Place sardines around the pizza, sprinkle capers and olives and place cherry tomato halves evenly. Drizzle pizza sauce over and add salt, chilli and oregano.
2. Cook for 7 to 10 minutes
3. When ready, cut up and serve with lemon wedges.

3 HOME SWEET HOME *Seafood*

NY salmon

The sesame seeds on the base of this pizza will toast in the oven while your pizza is cooking giving you a really nice nutty and crunchy base.

1 basic pizza dough ball
2 tablespoons sesame seeds
    (for rolling out the dough)
1 teaspoon garlic, finely chopped
90 g mozzarella, grated
70 g smoked salmon, sliced
30 g fresh leek, cut into 1 cm slices
60 g cream cheese, cut into small cubes
pinch of salt

50 ml whole egg mayonnaise (p136)
1 teaspoon fresh chives, chopped
1 lemon, cut into wedges

Pre-heat oven to 220°C

1. Before you start to roll out your dough ball, place sesame seeds on your bench. Put your dough ball on top of the seeds and use the palm of your hand to flatten the dough into the sesame seeds, then start to roll out your pizza dough ball to size. Try not to use too much flour on your bench, you are trying to press the seeds into the base as you roll it to size.

2. Sprinkle garlic over the sesame seed pizza base and top with mozzarella. Place slivers of smoked salmon and cubes of cream cheese evenly around, then top with leek and a pinch of salt.

3. Cook for 7 to 10 minutes.

4. When ready cut, swirl whole egg mayonnaise over, sprinkle the chives and squeeze lemon on pizza before eating.

3 HOME SWEET HOME *Seafood*

Nathan & Nat & prawn McManus

AKA 'Bogans by the beach'. This is for my mate Shaun. I know it started as a joke by Nathan & Nat taking the piss out of you, but I got to thinking and after a few failed attempts I found my inner Shaun and came up with a Reef & Beef pizza. This one's for you champ.

1 basic pizza dough ball – rolled, rested & ready
1 teaspoon garlic, finely chopped
90 g mozzarella, grated
70 g (8) large raw prawns, shelled and de-veined
1 fresh smoked chorizo sausage (not dried), in bite-sized pieces
50 g roasted red capsicum, sliced
30 g peas (fresh or thawed)
3 tablespoons cream sauce (p166)

1 teaspoon fresh parsley, chopped
balsamic glaze
1 lemon, cut into wedges

Pre-heat oven to 220°C

1. Sprinkle garlic over the pizza base then top with mozzarella. Place your prawns and bite-sized chorizo pieces evenly on the pizza. Top with red capsicum and sprinkle with peas. Drizzle with cream sauce.

2. Cook for 7 to 10 minutes.

3. When ready, cut into eight pieces, swirl the balsamic glaze over and sprinkle with parsley. Serve with lemon wedges.

3 HOME SWEET HOME *Seafood*

Creamy satay prawns

SATAY SAUCE

2 garlic cloves
140 g roasted, unsalted peanuts
6 spring onions, white part only
2 lemon grass stalks, roughly chopped
2 small red chillies, stalk chopped off
$1\frac{1}{2}$ tablespoon peanut oil
1 teaspoon fresh coriander leaves
375 ml coconut cream
1 teaspoon turmeric
1 teaspoon sea salt

PIZZA

1 basic pizza dough ball – rolled, rested & ready
1 teaspoon garlic, finely chopped
90 g mozzarella, grated
100 g (10) large raw prawns, shelled & de-veined
3 tablespoons, satay sauce
60 g white onion, thinly sliced
60 g roasted red capsicum, sliced
$1\frac{1}{2}$ tablespoon coconut milk
pinch of salt

30 g roasted peanut, coarsely crushed
1 teaspoon fresh coriander leaves
1 lemon, cut into wedges

Pre-heat oven to 220°C

1. Place all your ingredients in a food processor and pulse till everything is finely chopped.

2. In a non-stick pan over a low to medium heat, cook till it comes to a gentle simmer – this should take about 3 minutes.

3. When the paste is simmering, turn off the heat and leave the sauce to cool down in the pan. When cool, place in a bowl, it's ready to use.

This sauce will keep for seven days in a sealed container in the fridge.

1. Mix prawns and satay sauce in a bowl and leave to sit for five minutes.

2. Sprinkle the garlic over the pizza base and top with mozzarella. Place your marinated prawns around the pizza, top with onion and capsicum, drizzle coconut milk over, and add a pinch of salt.

3. Cook for 7 to 10 minutes.

4. When ready, cut into eight and finish off with roasted peanuts, fresh coriander leaves and serve with a lemon wedge.

VEGETARIAN

So many starring toppings and so many pizzas! Mushrooms! Chick peas! Haloumi! Asparagus! Eggplant! And don't forget the gluten-free recipe on page 16, the Teglia with porcini mushrooms on page 11, or the simple (but difficult!) Napoletana STG on page 19, and, of course, the wholesome Beverly Hills Grove Farmers Market pizza on page 101. There are some real flavours here! And the delicious Blue Monday with pear and blue vein cheese makes a wonderful intermezzo between mains and dessert

3 HOME SWEET HOME *Vegetarian*

Mushroom Records

This pizza is all about mushrooms and about getting the freshest mushrooms you can find and making them the star of the pizza.

If you can't find the mushrooms I have listed, use whatever you can find.

MUSHROOM MIX

1 cup button mushrooms, sliced
1 cup field mushrooms, sliced
1 cup shitake mushrooms, sliced
1 tablespoon parsley, chopped
1 clove of garlic, minced
$\frac{1}{2}$ small red chilli
1 teaspoon rosemary, chopped
pinch of salt
pinch of pepper

PIZZA

1 basic pizza dough ball – rolled, rested & ready
1 cup low-fat mozzarella, grated
3 cups mushroom mix
$\frac{1}{2}$ cup feta cheese, diced (only use full-cream, the low-fat won't melt)

1 really big handful of rocket leaves in an olive oil-vinegar-salt dressing

Pre-heat oven to 220°C

1   Mix the sliced mushrooms with the parsley, garlic, chilli, rosemary, salt and pepper and leave to marinate for 5 minutes.

1   Spread mozzarella over pizza base, place your mushroom mix evenly over the cheese and crumble the feta on top.

2   Cook for 7 to 10 minutes.

3   When ready, cut into 12 pieces, place on serving plate and top with the rocket leaves and serve immediately.

With all the flavour from the mushrooms and the crunch from the rocket on this pizza, you are simply in heaven.

3 HOME SWEET HOME *Vegetarian*

Tame Impala

This vegetarian pizza stars a very underused cheese on pizza, haloumi. Haloumi is a cheese from Cyprus and it is a staple for the Cypriots – they eat it for breakfast grilled with fresh fruit. The cheese does not fully melt into goo, it retains it's shape well, which gives it a great bite. As I was trialling the recipe I thought the pizza needed something to balance the flavours of cream sauce with garlic and that's where the green 'Impala' peppercorns come in. The peppercorn is in brine and does not have the heat of black peppercorn, it is soft like a caper but once it goes in the oven, it gets toasted and pops as you eat it and then you get this slight warmth as well.

Tame Impala is a great Perth band that comes in to the Leederville pizzeria. I really love their music so I wanted to name a pizza after the band, but with Tame and Impala as my ingredients, well, let's just say I had no chance. So I made something up, a complete lie! There is no such thing as Green 'Impala' Peppercorns, but as you read it, it does sound like they are real. Sorry guys, I hope this is cool with you; you're going to love this pizza.

CREAM SAUCE (BASIC)

25 g butter
$\frac{1}{2}$ teaspoon extra virgin olive oil
$\frac{1}{4}$ red onion, finely chopped
125 ml cream
125 ml sour cream
pinch of salt
pinch of pepper

1. In a small pot, on medium heat, put in the butter and extra virgin olive oil. Cook the onions until they are soft and translucent – you do not want to brown them (if you do it will give a strong cooked onion flavour and you are not after that).
2. When the onions are ready, add the cream and stir for about one minute. Add sour cream and stir till the sauce is gently simmering away.
3. Add salt and pepper to taste.
4. Take off heat and let it cool down before drizzling onto pizza.

    This sauce will keep for seven days in an airtight container in the fridge. It is also great mixed in with your favourite pasta.

PIZZA

1 basic pizza dough ball – rolled, rested & ready
1 tablespoon garlic, finely chopped
80 g mozzarella, grated
90 g haloumi, cut into eight slices
2 teaspoons green 'Impala' peppercorns
2 teaspoons Greek oregano
    (if not available normal is fine)
4 tablespoons cream sauce
pinch of salt
pinch of pepper

1 lemon, cut into wedges – this brings the finishing touch!

Pre-heat oven to 220°C

1. Spread garlic on the pizza base and sprinkle mozzarella up to the crust. Place the eight slices of haloumi evenly around the pizza from the centre to the crust, so that when cut, the haloumi cheese is in the middle of each slice.
2. Sprinkle the green peppercorns and oregano evenly over the pizza. Add a pinch of salt and pepper.
3. Drizzle cream sauce around the pizza making two rings: one on the outside and one in the middle. This way the melted cream sauce will spread evenly across the pizza.
4. Cook for 7 to 10 minutes.
5. Cut into eight pieces and place a lemon wedge on each for your guests to squeeze onto their slice.

3 HOME SWEET HOME *Vegetarian*

Asparagus in herb butter and gruyere

This pizza has no sauce, but the butter placed on the pizza when it has been cooked starts to melt releasing garlic and parsley flavours and becomes the sauce. You end up with a creamy buttery taste combining with the nutty earthy flavour of the Gruyere.

Note: only make this pizza when asparagus are in season – canned asparagus are no good.

1 pizza dough ball – rolled, rested & ready
8 asparagus spears, snapped and the ends peeled then blanched for three minutes (this pizza needs to be cut into 8 pieces if you are going to cut into 12 pieces, use 12 asparagus spears)
1 teaspoon garlic, finely chopped
50 g mozzarella, grated
50 g Gruyere, thinly sliced

3 teaspoons of garlic butter (p122)
1 teaspoon thyme
pinch of white pepper

Pre-heat oven to 220°C

1. Sprinkle garlic and then mozzarella evenly over the base, place your asparagus evenly around the pizza like the big hand on a clock, pointing from the edge to the middle, then place the Gruyere evenly over the asparagus making sure each piece of pizza will get some.

2. Cook for 7 to 10 minutes.

3. When cooked, cut into eight pieces, dollop garlic butter around pizza, sprinkle with thyme and white pepper then serve.

3 HOME SWEET HOME *Vegetarian*

Saha

SPICY TOMATO SAUCE

3 small green chillies, de-seeded and cut into chunks
pinch of salt
100 ml extra virgin olive oil
1 garlic clove
400 g tin whole peeled tomatoes
50 ml red wine vinegar

PIZZA

1 basic pizza dough ball – rolled, rested & ready
180 g grilled eggplant
1 tablespoon garlic, finely chopped
1 teaspoon cumin
1 teaspoon mixed spice
1 teaspoon paprika
pinch of salt
80 g mozzarella, grated
3 tablespoons spicy tomato sauce

3 tablespoons natural yoghurt
1 tablespoon toasted pine nuts
1 teaspoon fresh mint leaves

Pre-heat oven to 220°C

1. Put all the ingredients in a blender and pulse till you get a smooth sauce.
2. Put the sauce into a pot over medium heat and stir until it starts to boil. Turn off and leave to cool down before using.

   This sauce can be made the day before and will keep for seven days in the fridge.

1. In a bowl place the grilled eggplant with garlic, cumin, mixed spice, paprika and salt. Mix and let it sit for 5 minutes.
2. Put the marinated eggplant onto the pizza base, sprinkle with mozzarella and swirl sauce all over.
3. Cook for 7 to 10 minutes.
4. When ready, cut up, put a dollop of yoghurt on each piece, sprinkle over toasted pine nuts and mint leaves and serve.

3 HOME SWEET HOME *Vegetarian*

Chick magnet

This pizza has a slight middle eastern twist with the zatar and the yoghurt, cumin, mixed spice and paprika.

Zatar is a Middle-Eastern spice mixture containing oregano, basil, thyme, saturejia, sesame seeds and dried sumac. It is available at all good specialty shops.

The sauce has a bite to it (vinegar) so there may only be chick peas on it, but there is a lot of depth and many flavours going on.

1 basic pizza dough ball – rolled, rested & ready
1 tablespoon garlic, finely chopped
80 g mozzarella, grated
200 g chick peas (from the can is alright)
1 teaspoon cumin
3 tablespoons spicy tomato sauce recipe (p170)
pinch of salt

sprinkle of parsley, chopped
3 tablespoons natural yoghurt
1 teaspoon zatar

Pre-heat oven to 220°C

1. Spread garlic on your pizza base then top with the mozzarella.
2. In a bowl place chick peas, cumin, tomato sauce and salt. Mix together, then sprinkle the marinated chick peas evenly over the pizza.
3. Cook for 7 to 10 minutes.
4. When cooked, cut into eight pieces and drizzle with yoghurt. Sprinkle over the zatar evenly, making sure it lands on the yoghurt. Top with parsley and serve.

3 HOME SWEET HOME *Vegetarian*

Blue Monday

This pizza has no sauce, as sometimes tomato pizza sauce can be overpowering. With this pizza it's all about flavours and textures, the caramelised pears, the sharp creamy blue cheese and the nutty crunch from the walnuts.

CANDIED WALNUTS

40 g walnut pieces
$\frac{1}{4}$ cup brown sugar

PIZZA

1 basic pizza dough ball – rolled, rested & ready
80 g mozzarella, grated
1 large pear – peeled, cored and sliced thinly
1 teaspoon brown sugar

65 g blue cheese
40 g candied walnuts
pinch of parsley, chopped

Pre-heat oven to 220°C

1. Place greaseproof paper on a flat tray.
2. Heat brown sugar in a non-stick pan on medium heat. When it starts to melt add the walnut pieces and stir. When the sugar starts to bubble take the pan off the heat and pour the mixture onto baking paper to cool.
3. When using on the pizza break into bite-sized pieces.

   Stores in an airtight container for up to seven days.

1. Sprinkle mozzarella evenly over base and place pears on top so they look like an open fan, sprinkle brown sugar over pear slices, place in oven.
2. Cook for 7 to 10 minutes.
3. When ready, cut up, crumble blue cheese over pears, place candied walnuts on each piece, sprinkle with parsley and serve.

DESSERT

People often come to my pizzaria to try a dessert pizza. They have heard about dessert pizzas, but can't quite believe it is possible to make them… or that they will taste good. Of course, they all find out that dessert pizzas are beyond delicious! In addition to my award-winning Strawberry fields dessert pizza on page 52, the Red velvet pizza I created for Liz on page 95, and the Blondie with homemade honeycomb on page 74, I have included some old and new favourites from my restaurant here. How about the good oldfashioned flavours of banoffee or sticky date pudding given a fresh twist onto a pizza? Or maybe try the Snowman or the Cherry pie or the Smudges or…

3 HOME SWEET HOME *Dessert*

Peanut butter banana

The creamy-nutty flavour of peanut butter combined with sweet bananas, salted peanuts and maple syrup is a match made in heaven.

1 basic pizza dough ball – rolled, rested & ready
3 tablespoons smooth peanut butter, at room temperature
1 banana, cut into 14 slices
1 tablespoon light brown sugar

$\frac{1}{2}$ cup dry-roasted, salted peanuts, crushed
1 tablespoon maple syrup

Pre-heat oven to 220°C

1. Spread peanut butter on prepared pizza dough. Top with banana slices, then place a pinch of brown sugar on top of each banana slice.

2. Cook for 7–10 minutes or until the edges are golden brown.

3. Remove pizza from oven, place on a serving tray, and cut into 12 slices. Sprinkle each slice with crushed peanuts and drizzle with maple syrup.

HOT TIP For a chocolate flavour replace the peanut butter with a choc-hazelnut spread like Nutella.

3 HOME SWEET HOME *Dessert*

Snowman

CHOCOLATE SAUCE

1 cup fresh cream
1 cup dark chocolate
1 cup milk chocolate

PIZZA

1 basic pizza dough ball – rolled, rested & ready
1 egg
90 ml coconut milk
70 g plain flour
½ teaspoon baking powder
pinch of salt
50 g shredded coconut

1 cup dark chocolate, chopped
3 tablespoons chocolate sauce
1 cup shredded coconut
2 scoops of ice-cream

Pre-heat oven to 220°C

1   In a thick-bottomed saucepan on a low heat, place the cream and chocolates. As the milk starts to heat up, the chocolate will start to melt. Use a whisk to gently mix until all the chocolate has melted and the chocolate sauce is simmering away, then turn off.

The chocolate sauce can be kept in the fridge for 14 days. It will go hard in the fridge so you will need to soften it either at room temperature, in the microwave or back on the stove – make sure you only heat it up until the chocolate sauce is runny enough to drizzle over the pizza.

1   In a bowl, whisk the egg and then whisk in the coconut milk. Add the flour, baking powder and salt and mix together, it should be a nice thick consistency. Add the shredded coconut and mix in, scoop out the mixture onto the pizza base and spread evenly around about 2 cm from the edge, the crust will help stop the mixture from running over the edge.

2   Bake for 7 to 10 minutes.

3   When ready cut into 12 pieces.

4   To decorate, cover the cooked and cut pizza with dark chocolate and half the shredded coconut. Place the two scoops of ice-cream on top of each other like a snowman in the middle of the pizza, then sprinkle the rest of the coconut over the snowman, drizzle the chocolate sauce over the snowman and around the pizza. You've got to work fast to get this right, but it is worth it!

There is a special way to eat this pizza: you need to have some of the snowman on a spoon going into your mouth at the same time as a slice of the pizza. DELISIOS.

Banoffee

TOFFEE SAUCE

90 g unsalted butter
1 cup soft brown sugar
2 tablespoons golden syrup
pinch salt
$\frac{2}{3}$ cup fresh cream

PIZZA

1 pizza dough ball – rolled, rested & ready
65 g unsalted butter, softened
$\frac{1}{2}$ cup caster sugar
$\frac{1}{2}$ teaspoon vanilla paste
1 egg
1 cup self raising flour
2 tablespoons toffee sauce
1 banana cut into 1 cm slices

icing sugar for dusting
dollop of thickened cream
3 tablespoons toffee sauce

1. In a non-stick pot on medium heat place butter, brown sugar, golden syrup and pinch of salt, stir till the sugar dissolves – this will take about three minutes.
2. Add the cream, and stir and cook for three minutes. The toffee sauce should be slightly thicker than honey – that's when you will know it's ready.

Pre-heat oven to 220°C

1. Place the butter and sugar into your mixing bowl and, using the flat paddle attachment, cream together on a medium speed for one minute, scrape down. Add the egg and mix for one minute, scrape down.
2. Add flour and vanilla paste and mix on a low speed for one minute, scrape down, then mix on a medium speed for another minute.
3. Remove bowl from mixer and spread over the pizza base. Spread two tablespoons of toffee sauce over and gently swirl the toffee into the batter to create a marble effect.
4. Place sliced banana evenly on the pizza and bake for 7 minutes.
5. When cooked, cut into eight pieces, decorate with a dusting of icing sugar, a dollop of cream in the middle, and a drizzle of toffee sauce. Serve ASAP!

3 HOME SWEET HOME *Dessert*

Cherry pie

CHERRY SYRUP

90 g unsalted butter
2 tablespoons corn syrup
1 cup caster sugar
$\frac{2}{3}$ cup maraschino cherry juice (you can buy maraschino cherries in a jar at the supermarket – that way you get the juice as well).

PIZZA

1 basic pizza dough ball – rolled, rested & ready
65 g softened unsalted butter
$\frac{1}{2}$ cup caster sugar
1 egg
$\frac{1}{2}$ teaspoon vanilla paste
35 ml juice from maraschino cherries
1 cup self raising flour
8 maraschino cherries with stem attached

icing sugar for dusting
1 scoops of vanilla bean ice-cream
1 maraschino cherries with stem attached
3 tablespoons cherry syrup

Pre-heat oven to 220°C

1. Place butter, corn syrup and sugar in a non-stick pot over medium heat. Stir till the sugar dissolves – this will take about three minutes.

2. Pour in the cherry juice, stir and cook for another three minutes. The cherry syrup should be thick like honey – that's when you know it's ready.

1. Cream together butter and sugar on medium speed for one minute then scrape down.

2. Add egg, vanilla and cherry juice then mix on a low speed for one minute and scrape down.

3. Add flour and mix on low speed for one minute, scrape down, then mix for two minutes on medium speed – the batter should have a pink colour thanks to the cherry juice.

4. Spread the batter evenly over the base. Place eight cherries so that each piece gets a cherry.

5. Cook for 7 minutes.

6. When ready, cut into eight pieces. Decorate with a dusting of icing sugar, dollop the ice-cream scoop in the middle of the pizza, place a cherry on top of the ice-cream then drizzle with three tablespoons of cherry syrup. Serve ASAP.

3 HOME SWEET HOME *Dessert*

Sticky fingers

CARAMEL SAUCE

1 cup brown sugar
300 ml thickened cream
½ teaspoon vanilla
60 g butter

PIZZA

1 basic pizza dough ball – rolled, rested & ready
125 g softened butter
½ cup brown sugar
¼ teaspoon vanilla
1 egg
1 cup self raising flour
¼ cup dates, pitted and chopped
¼ cup white chocolate bits

icing sugar for dusting
1 scoop vanilla ice-cream
¼ cup dates, pitted and chopped
¼ cup white chocolate bits
1½ tablespoons caramel sauce

Pre-heat oven to 220°C

1. Melt the butter in a small saucepan with a thick base on medium heat.
2. Whisk in the cream, add the brown sugar and vanilla and continue whisking until the mixture starts to bubble. When it turns thick and gooey take the saucepan off the heat and let it cool down before using the sauce on your pizza.

   This sauce will keep for seven days in an airtight container in the fridge.

1. In a mixing bowl with a whisk attachment – or in a bowl with a hand whisk – mix the butter and brown sugar until the colour lightens.
2. Add the vanilla and the egg and whisk together till smooth.
3. Incorporate the flour, making sure there are no lumps. Add the dates and chocolate and fold in gently.
4. Spread onto the pizza base and cook for 7 to 10 minutes.
5. When ready cut into 12 pieces and dust with icing sugar. Place ice-cream scoops in the middle of pizza and sprinkle dates and chocolate all over. Drizzle with caramel sauce and serve ASAP.

3 HOME SWEET HOME *Dessert*

Pizza smudges

Cooking dessert pizzas in a really hot wood-fired oven is not easy; nearly all my dessert pizza recipes will not work in a wood-fired oven, as they require precise weight and measurement and baking at a consistent heat of 250°C for seven minutes. That temperature and cooking time are unrealistic in a roaring hot 350°C to 400°C wood-fired oven. What to do? It's easy and quick – pizza smudges.

Here are a few examples of some pizza smudges that I have made. You can follow these to get the idea of how to do them and then make up your own.

Passionfruit curd smudged on a base and topped with fresh blueberries

Nougat spread with fresh raspberries (be careful: the high sugar content in the nougat spread will burn your mouth if you eat it straight away, so let it cool a bit before serving)

Tinned caramel smudged on base, chopped pecan nuts, peach pieces

Hazelnut spread smudged on base, strawberries and desiccated coconut

Custard smudged on base with apricot pieces and a sprinkle of brown sugar

Lemon curd topped with blueberries

Custard smudge with marshmallows (the marshmallows will burn like toasted marshmallows which is great, but they will also burn you, so let it cool before you serve it).

Or you can use any combination you like.

I finish off my smudges with a dusting of icing sugar, a scoop of ice-cream or a dollop of freshly whipped cream.

Dessert pizza smudges will cook in about three minutes in a wood-fired oven; all you are doing is cooking your pizza base and then it's ready.

Pizza smudges are a great way to end a pizza party. Everyone gets to be creative and put flavours together for everybody else to try. The only problem you'll have is that you and your friends will be so full at the end of it that they can't move, while all the kids will be on a happy sugar-high!

189

TILL NEXT TIME ...

What I really love about what I do is that I can keep finding new ways of making pizzas: new flavours, new types of dough, new combinations. And with every trip I take, I encounter other pizza lovers who share their ideas as I share mine. It is this great big pizza family, cooking and competing around the world, and we all want the same thing: to make great pizza. So to the wonderful people I've met on my travels around the world: thanks for your time, recipes, knowledge and friendship, and thank you to Anita Lee for capturing some of those travel moments on film.

I couldn't have made this book without the help of a lot of people – Theo & Co. just keeps on growing! To all the Little Caesars pizzeria staff, from our central kitchen to the office, dishwasher, pizza maker, personal assistants and everything in-between, thank you for putting up with me and for delivering the goods every day, day after day, you are the '& Co.' and you guys make me proud to know my recipes are in safe hands when I leave to travel. To my customers – you keep wanting to try new things, and I get to make them; thank you!

To my friends at UWA Publishing – you turn my scribbles and ideas into fantastic books: you girls rock! And a big thank you to all the recipe testers who dedicated time trying to work out what was in my head and making it work on paper, and to the Zesti team for building such a great oven. Also big big thanks to my friend and photographer, Craig Kinder – you make my food look as good as it tastes, and to Paul and his girls, Marie and Scarlett, for working side by side with me, supporting and protecting me: thank you!

To my families – Kalogeracos family, Ioannou family, Filgoni family, Saraceni family, Bird family – I always drop into family gathering and take off way too early to go to work, but I cherish those moments with you.

And, finally, to my wife Elizabeth and my son Chaz-rae: you are my everything xxx.

The perfect pizza? It's somewhere. There are so many places I haven't yet visited, and so many foods and flavours I haven't yet tried. But I will continue my search, and I'll keep making pizzas and I'll let you know what I find. Till then: cook, eat, share and enjoy with your friends and family!

Big love

Theo

RECIPES

Recipes marked [w] for wood-fired oven or [g] for gas oven are best cooked in that type oven. Those pizzas that only need to be cooked at 220°C can also be cooked in a domestic oven; and many pizzas can be cooked in the counter-top oven which, although its set temperature is 200°C, will often work well because it heats from both the bottom and the top.

PIZZA DOUGH
Basic 33
Chicago deep dish 104
Classica 4
Napoltana [w] 19
New York 64
San Fran sourdough 80
Senza glutine (gluten-free) 15
Teglia 8
Upside-down 72
Wholemeal (100% and 70%) 96

SAUCE
Basic pizza sauce 33
BBQ 127
Chicago deep dish tomato 106
Classica 4
Cream sauce (basic) 166
Satay 160
Sour cream hollandaise 113
Spicy tomato 170
STG San Marzano 19
Upside-down tomato 72

PIZZA
Asparagus in herb butter and Gruyere 169
BBQ plate 127
Beverly Hills Grove Farmers Market [w, g] 101
Birds of Tokyo 135
Black box 57
BLAT 136
Blue Monday 175
Chicago deep dish spinach [g] 106
Chicken & leek 140
Chick magnet 173
Cinnamon Girl 143
Creamy satay prawns 160
Eggs Florentine 113
Fennel sausage (classica) [w] 7
Flaming lips 153
Gluten-free vegetarian 16
Green eggs & ham 114
Jebediah 116
Kangaroo and pomegranate [w, g] 132
Mushroom Records 165
Napoletana STG 20
Nathan & Nat & prawn McManus 159
New York-style clam [w, g] 67
New York upside-down [g] 72
NY salmon 156
Porcini mushrooms (teglia) [g] 11
Pork & sage 144
Pork star 147
Portuguese chicken 148
Puttanesca 154
Roast chicken burrito 131
Saha 170
Sicilian Swordfish (teglia) [g] 12
Slow-cooked pork belly & white wine onions on sourdough [w, g] 83
Speck & peas 139
Tame Impala 166
Tribeca [w, g] 71
Wood-fired pork loin with balsamic tears 61

DESSERT PIZZA
Banoffee 183
Blondie 74
Cherry Pie 185
Peanut butter banana 179
Red velvet 95
Smudges [w] 189
Snowman 180
Sticky fingers 186
Strawberry Fields 52

OTHER – SAVOURY
Achiote-marinated chicken 128
Basil-cashew pesto 99
Biga 80
Butter 121
Caramelised onions
  Black box 57
  BBQ plate 127
Clams 67
Cooked mushrooms
  Teglia 11
  Black box 57
Garlic bread 122
Garlic butter 122
Guacamole 131
Marinated zucchini 99
Mushroom mix 165
Oven roasted beetroot 99
Pico de gallo 131
Pork mince 147
Roasted red capsicum 98
Roasted butternut pumpkin 99
Slow-cooked pork belly 83
Spiced kangaroo fillets 132
Spicy tomato salsa 128
Steamed and spiced baby spinach 113
Whole-egg mayonnaise 136
Wood-fired pork loin [w] 61

OTHER – SWEET
Candied walnuts 175
Caramel sauce 186
Cherry syrup 185
Chocolate sauce 180
Cream cheese icing 92
Easy olive oil ice-cream 89
Frangipane mix 52
Honeycomb 74
Red velvet cupcakes 92
Strawberry jam 52
Toffee sauce 183
White brownie mix 74

INDEX

MEASUREMENTS

1 teaspoon equals 5 g
1 tablespoon equals 20 g
1 cup equals 225 g

INGREDIENTS

almond meal 52
asparagus 169
avocado 131, 136

baby spinach 71, 106, 113, 114
bacon 71, 127, 136, 140
balsamic 11, 58, 61, 78, 99, 143, 159
banana 79, 179, 183
beetroot 58, 61, 69, 91, 92, 99, 101
blue cheese 27, 175

capsicum, roasted 16, 27, 98, 101, 148, 159, 160
cashew nuts 99
chick peas 173
chicken 15, 43, 44, 57, 71, 91, 127, 128, 131, 135, 140, 143, 148
chilli 128, 131, 153, 154, 160, 165, 170
chocolate 179, 180, 186
chorizo 159
cinnamon 43, 79, 116, 143
clams 67, 78
coconut
   cream 160
   milk 160, 180
   shredded 79, 180, 191
coriander, fresh 128, 131, 160
cream 57, 74, 85, 86, 89, 121, 166, 180, 183, 186, 191
cream cheese 79, 92, 95, 156

dates 186

eggplant 15, 170

feta 165

haloumi 27, 166
ham 114, 127

ice-cream 52, 116, 180, 185, 186, 191

kangaroo 132

leek 86, 140, 156

mayonnaise
   Japanese 135, 153
   whole-egg 114, 136, 156
mint 52, 170
mozzarella, smoked 26, 27, 44, 55, 57
mushrooms 1, 11, 15, 16, 57, 59, 79, 86, 91, 165

olives 12, 78, 91, 154

parmesan 1, 25, 26, 57, 78, 79, 91, 99, 106
peanut butter 179
peas 86, 139, 159
pecorino 1, 11, 63, 67
pesto 12, 57, 85, 99
pine nuts 57, 170
pork 43, 44, 58, 61, 77, 83, 144, 147
potato, sweet 143, 144, 147
prawns 15, 159, 160
pumpkin 85, 99, 101

rocket 1, 11, 78, 79, 85, 165
romano 63, 67, 72
rosemary 25, 43, 86, 127, 165
sage 86, 144
sardines 154
scamorza 69, 71
sesame seeds 28, 122, 135, 156, 173
sour cream 113, 166
speck 79, 86, 139
strawberries 52, 191

thyme 86, 140, 169, 173
tomato
   cherry 16, 78, 154
   fresh 1, 3, 27, 28, 33, 85, 128, 131, 136
   tinned 3, 4, 19, 72, 106, 128, 170
tuna 153

vinegar 127, 165, 170

white wine 11, 67, 77, 83, 140

yoghurt
   Greek 101
   natural 170, 173

zucchini 15, 16, 91, 99, 101

First published in 2012
by UWA Publishing
Crawley, Western Australia 6009
www.uwap.uwa.edu.au

UWAP is an imprint of UWA Publishing,
a division of The University of Western Australia

This book is copyright. Apart from any fair dealing for the purpose private study, research, criticism or review, as permitted under the *Copyright Act 1968*, no part may be reproduced by any process without written permission. Enquiries should be made to the publisher.

Copyright © Theo Kalogeracos 2012

The moral right of the author has been asserted

Local Photography by Craig Kinder @ F22 Photography
Food styled by Kate Pickard
CMYK colour conversion by Henrik Tivid
Edited by Anne Ryden
Design and typeset by Anna Maley-Fadgyas
Printed by Imago

National Library of Australia Cataloguing-in-Publication entry

   Kalogeracos, Theodore.

   Theo take 2 : the search for the perfect pizza continues / Theo Kalogeracos.

   9781742583532 (pbk.)

   Includes index.

        Pizza.
        Cooking, Italian.
        Cooking, American.
        Stoves, Wood--Design and construction.

   641.8248